An Invitation to Shabbat

• • • • • • • • • • • •

A Beginner's Guide to Weekly Celebration

• • • • • • • • • • • •

Ruth Perelson

A Project of the
Union of American Hebrew Congregations
Department of Education
and the William and Lottie Daniel
Department of Outreach

UAHC Press
New York, New York

Come, Let Us Welcome Shabbat (CLUWS), a peer-led process, was initiated and developed as an adult education project by Ruth Perelson and the CLUWS Committee, under the auspices of Central Synagogue, New York City. CLUWS has received the Or Ami Award of the Women of Reform Judaism.

The Union of American Hebrew Congregations Department of Education and the William and Lottie Daniel Department of Outreach, in cooperation with the UAHC Committee on the Jewish Family and the UAHC Commission on Religious Living, invites individuals and congregations to initiate Shabbat home observance, as presented in *An Invitation to Shabbat.*

An Invitation to Shabbat is designed to help you prepare for the special experience of Welcoming the Sabbath—*Kabbalat Shabbat*—and celebrating it with prayer, songs, conversation, and a festive meal. Once you have been initiated into this period of sacred time, we urge you to deepen your involvement with and commitment to Shabbat observance by acquiring and using the prayer books and ritual guides published by the Central Conference of American Rabbis and the educational resources available from the Union of American Hebrew Congregations, which are listed in the Bibliography on pages 68–74.

Library of Congress Cataloging-in-Publication Data

Perelson, Ruth
An invitation to Shabbat : a beginner's guide to weekly celebration/Ruth Perelson.
p. cm.
"A Project of the Union of American Hebrew Congregations Department of Education."
Includes bibliographical references.
ISBN 0-8074-0611-2 (pbk.)
1. Sabbath. 2. Reform Judaism—Customs and practices. I. Union of American Hebrew Congregations. Dept. of Education. II. Title.
BM685.P44 1997
296.4'1—dc21   96—48518
                                                              CIP

This book is printed on acid-free paper.

DEDICATION

To Rabbi Sheldon Zimmerman, who as
scholar, mentor, and dear friend has shown
that teshuvah—*one's "turning" or "return" to*
Judaism—is not as difficult as it may appear.

ACKNOWLEDGMENTS

More than Israel has kept the Sabbath, the Sabbath has kept Israel.

—AHAD HA-AM

Thanks go to the pioneering CLUWS workshops' teaching team of Central Synagogue, New York City: Wendy Botuck, Jo David, Joanne Doades, Barbara and Bob Jayson, Bud Lustbader, Marion Lustbader (may her memory be for a blessing), Bernie Silverman, Gloria Silverman, Paul Stone, Neil Yerman, and Civia Zoe.

Thanks also to my loving husband, Sam, and our children, Lois and Stewart Perelson Gross and Lila and Keith Adwar, who, by their presence at our Shabbat table, have greatly expanded our capacity for loving celebration.

And special thanks to our granddaughters, Hannah Perelson Gross, born April 30, 1992, and Sarah Alice Perelson Gross, born November 1, 1994, who love to celebrate Shabbat as much as they love to celebrate their birthdays. They and all the children of future generations remind us always of God's presence in our lives.

—RUTH PERELSON

We are indebted to the following devoted members of UAHC commissions, task force groups, committees, and congregations, who have helped reveal the beauty of Sabbath holiness: Rabbi Les Bronstein; Rabbi Daniel Freelander; Harvey Gordon, MD; Brooke Harris; Rabbi Lawrence Hoffman; Emita Levy; Lillian Maltzer; Mildred Ross; Esther Saritzky; Daniel S. Schechter; Cantor Benjie Ellen Schiller; Naomi Gale Silverman; Alayne Zatulove; Rabbi Sheldon Zimmerman; and Rabbi Bernard Zlotowitz.

New friends have spent much time and effort helping us revise this book. We wish to thank the staff of the UAHC Press for their assistance, especially Kathy Parnass, Cara Schlesinger, and Elyn Wollensky. We also owe a great debt to the director of the Outreach Department, Dru Greenwood, and the following Outreach coordinators from UAHC regions around the country: Arlene Chernow, Robin Farquhar, Linda Gordon, and Linda Steigman; Antoinette Matlins, South Woodstock, Vermont; Tracy Nathan; Andee Hochman; Ariel Friedlander and Leon Morris, rabbinic students, HUC-JIR, New York; and Rabbi Brian Zimmerman, Temple Beth Ami, Rockville, Maryland.

CONTENTS

What Shabbat Means to Me 48

This book was written for you

- If you want to "stop the clock" each week to experience renewal.

- If you want to bring Judaism into your life.

- If you want to embark on a spiritual journey through Judaism.

- If you want to identify and bond with your universal Jewish family, past, present, and future.

- If you want to bring God into your consciousness.

- If you want to acquire a Jewish perspective of love and togetherness.

Have you been too busy or do you consider yourself too unprepared to celebrate Shabbat? Have you any idea what *Kabbalat Shabbat* should be like? Perhaps the last time you experienced Shabbat at home was as a child in your parents' or grandparents' house. Or perhaps you are one of the many people who have never experienced *Kabbalat Shabbat*.

If you would like to be able to welcome Shabbat but do not know where to begin, this book was written for you, regardless of your age, stage in life, or prior knowledge of Judaism. It was written for you if you are a bat/bar mitzvah, a high school student, a college student, newly engaged, newly wed, married, single, divorced, widowed, a parent, a grandparent, childless, gay, lesbian, heterosexual, born Jewish, new to Judaism, or contemplating Judaism. It was written to empower you in an egalitarian environment. Now that we are no longer bound by the traditional gender roles, we encourage you to sample all the rituals.

An Invitation to Shabbat was designed to provide you with the first steps in building the confidence to experience *Kabbalat Shabbat*—Welcoming the Sabbath—as a joyous celebration. My assumption is that you have no previous experience. My goal is to help you reach an "I can do this weekly" confidence level. This book is for the beginner who wants to learn how to sway to the peaceful rhythm of Shabbat.

What does *Kabbalat Shabbat* encompass?

- *Kabbalat Shabbat* encourages you to experience Jewish ritual each week.

- *Kabbalat Shabbat* is quality time that you set aside for the appreciation of yourself, your loved ones, your friends, and your environment.

Shabbat is both private and public. It provides an opportunity for introspection, prayer, and study.

- *Kabbalat Shabbat* is many occasions rolled into one unique day. It is your weekly birthday party for the world; a "taste" of the perfect messianic World to Come; a celebration of the joys of living, loving, and creativity; a time to sing!

- *Kabbalat Shabbat* presents an opportunity for you to begin learning about the concept of fulfilling God's commandments to remember— *zachor*—and observe—*shamor*—the Sabbath.

- *Kabbalat Shabbat* encourages you to take your time developing a ritual with which you are comfortable. The evolving process of celebration can be compared to designing an article of clothing: You have to tailor it to suit your own needs.

- *Kabbalat Shabbat* requires commitment. Be prepared to make changes in your routine so that you can dedicate time to this major change.

- *Kabbalat Shabbat* needs to become a part of your consciousness. Its rituals can enrich and redefine the meaning of your activities during the rest of the week.

As you use this book, please remember that everyone was once a beginner. There are many people who would be happy to help you. No question is too small or silly. Your congregational family of rabbis, cantors, educators, and friends can all serve as wonderful consultants.

SHABBAT SHALOM.
RUTH

What Is It All About?

· · · · · · · · · · ◆ · · · · · · · · ·

Shabbat is the most important time of the week as it offers a haven … to appreciate the beauties of life.… The Sabbath itself is a sanctuary that we build, a sanctuary in time.

—ABRAHAM JOSHUA HESCHEL
THE SABBATH

The Spectrum of Traditions
An Overview

Remember the Sabbath day and keep it holy. Six days you shall labor and do all your work, but the seventh day is a Sabbath of *Adonai* your God: You shall not do any work—you, your son or daughter, your male or female slave, or your cattle, or the stranger who is within your settlements. For in six days *Adonai* made heaven and earth and sea, and all that is in them, and God rested on the seventh day; therefore, *Adonai* blessed the seventh day and hallowed it.

—EXODUS 20:8-11

Observe the Sabbath day and keep it holy, as *Adonai* your God has commanded you.... Remember that you were a slave in the land of Egypt and *Adonai* your God freed you from there with a mighty hand and an outstretched arm; therefore, *Adonai* your God has commanded you to observe the Sabbath day.

—DEUTERONOMY 5:12,15

Shabbat embodies the essence of Judaism, symbolizing the relationship of the Jewish people to God and to humankind. So important is the Sabbath that it alone of all Jewish festivals is mentioned in the creation story and in the Ten Commandments; not even Yom Kippur shares that privilege....

By referring to the Exodus from Egypt, the fourth commandment reminds Jews of their covenant with God, the lessons of their history, and the evils of slavery. The Torah, recognizing the ease with which humans enslave themselves to ideas, routine, and each other, provided the Sabbath as a weekly counterforce. One who never experiences freedom may neither yearn nor strive for it, but the slave who tastes freedom even one day a week will eventually rebel against enslavement.

—*KEEPING POSTED*, VOL. XXVII, NO. 2

The Sabbath is a twenty-five-hour sanctuary in time within which you are free to refrain from your daily obligations. All Jewish observances begin the evening before the day we commemorate. For Orthodox Jews, Shabbat begins eighteen minutes before sunset on Friday. For Reform Jews, it usually begins when everyone is ready to sit down together at the dinner table and light the candles. This special time that you have set aside is distinct from any other part of the week. The ideal mood is festive but mellow.

The traditional celebration of the Sabbath begins prior to sunset on Friday evening with the lighting of the Sabbath candles and concludes on Saturday evening with the *Havdalah* service, which is conducted after the sighting of three stars in the sky. The *Havdalah* service separates the sanctity of the Sabbath from the activities of the rest of the week.

What happens in the traditional home and in the synagogue between that time?

The traditional Jew begins the celebration of the Sabbath with the *Kabbalat Shabbat* service on Friday evening in the synagogue. This service consists of the regular *Ma'ariv* (evening) service plus additional prayers. Traditionally, men attend this service, while women, who have already lit the candles at home, await their return from synagogue for the prepared Shabbat meal. The meal is festive and is combined with study of the Torah portion of the week. There is usually a lively discussion of the portion's teachings and much singing of *zemirot*—Shabbat songs—around the table.

On Saturday morning, the entire family goes to synagogue and then has a Shabbat lunch at home. The afternoon is spent visiting, resting, and/or studying. A third meal—called *se'udah shelishit*—is eaten in the late afternoon. *Havdalah* can be conducted at home or with the community after the evening service in the synagogue.

What happens in Reform communities during the twenty-five-hour sanctuary period? Within Reform communities, the *Kabbalat Shabbat* service is held in the synagogue at varied times. In some communities, an evening service conducted early three times a month may be coupled with a later service conducted once a month. In other communities, the Friday night *Kabbalat Shabbat* service is conducted after eight in the evening so that people can welcome the Sabbath at dinner in their home and then with the larger community.

The ideal is not to engage in labor of any kind on Shabbat. Another ideal is to combine home celebration with temple attendance so that prayer and study occur in the company of community.

The twenty-five-hour cycle may be structured in the following way:

Friday evening	*Kabbalat Shabbat* at home and in the temple.
Saturday morning	Worship services.
	Torah study at the temple.
Saturday lunch	With family and/or company.

Saturday afternoon	Family/friend togetherness in a nonworking, noncompetitive environment.
	Se'udah shelishit: a traditional third meal or late-day snack.
	Havdalah: saying good-bye to Shabbat.

The Friday evening temple service is marked by a mood of joyous anticipation. It is different from other evening services because it begins with a preliminary service called *Kabbalat Shabbat*—Welcoming the Sabbath. This service is of relatively recent origin, having been introduced by the kabbalistic scholars of Safed in the middle of the sixteenth century. It was first set down in the *Seder Hayom* by Rabbi Moshe ibn Machir in 1599. After that, it spread to Jewish communities throughout the world, gradually gaining acceptance as an integral part of the Friday evening service.

The Roots of Shabbat

Bernard M. Zlotowitz

According to traditional Jewish belief, the Sabbath has its origin in God's divine command to observe the seventh day as a day of rest and sanctification. Scholars, on the other hand, are divided in their opinion concerning the origin of the Sabbath, although they all agree that it was borrowed from another culture. Some scholars contend that its origin is Babylonian. The Babylonians believed that the seventh, fourteenth, twenty-first, and twenty-eighth days of the month (following the phases of the moon) were evil days and, therefore, the physician, the oracular priest, and the king ceased all labor on those days. The cessation of work on the day they called *Sabattu* was based upon fear and had no relation to the biblical concept of the Sabbath as a day of rest, joy, and refreshment of the soul.

Other scholars contend that the Hebrews borrowed the concept from the Canaanites, whose primitive agricultural calendar was based on a seven-day week. The Canaanites regarded the number seven to be evil and unlucky, a potential source of ill fortune to be avoided at all costs. They viewed this final day of the week as one on which evil spirits abounded and, therefore, as a day on which human labor would not prosper.

The ancient Hebrews, however, transformed this negative character of the seventh day into one of joy, refraining from labor because it was a day of gladness of the spirit. None of the scholarly theories explain how and why the Jews, who were supposed to have borrowed the Sabbath from the Canaanites or Babylonians, accomplished this transformation.

Traditionally, Judaism teaches that the Sabbath was unique to ancient Hebrew culture and was not influenced by others. It contends that the Sabbath as a day of rest and joy is our special contribution to the world, a gift from the Jewish people to all humankind.

Many of the Sabbath rituals originated during the period of the Talmud. Elaborating on the Bible's general and often vague Sabbath prohibitions, the Talmud sought to formalize and thereby protect the observance of Shabbat, listing in detail all acts prohibited on that day. To the thirty-nine types of forbidden labor, which are modeled on the tasks performed by the priests in constructing the Tabernacle (Exodus 31), the rabbis added "fences" designed to minimize the likelihood of violating the Sabbath. For example, since the rabbis interpreted the Bible to prohibit writing on Shabbat, they also outlawed the carrying of a writing implement on the seventh day.

In the process of clarifying biblical law, the rabbis sought to lessen its severity. For example, the Bible states, "You shall kindle no fire in all your habitations on the day of Shabbat." (Exodus 35:3) A strict interpretation would have prohibited the use of fire or heat in any form for the duration of the Sabbath. The rabbis, however, permitted the use of fire for light or heat so long as it had been kindled before the onset of Shabbat.

These laws, collected in the Talmud, formed the blueprint for Shabbat observance. Elaborating both on what should not be done in violation of the Sabbath and what should be done to enhance it, the Talmud provides laws concerning travel, work, lighting candles, eating, praying, caring for the sick, sexual relations, childbirth, circumcision, and virtually every other aspect of human endeavor that might occur on the Sabbath.

—*KEEPING POSTED*, VOL. XXVII, NO. 2

Shabbat

Linda Steigman

An ardent admirer once asked a great pianist, "How do you handle the notes as well as you do?" The artist answered, "The notes I handle no better than many pianists, but the pauses between the notes … ah, that is where the art resides."

In great living, as in great music, the art may be in the pauses. Surely one of the enduring contributions that Judaism has made to the art of living is the Shabbat, "the pause between the notes." And it is to the Shabbat that we must look if we are to restore to our lives the sense of serenity and sanctity that Shabbat offers in such joyous abundance.

—*LIKRAT SHABBAT*

The Sabbath is mentioned in the Torah on four separate occasions. In Genesis 2:1-3, we learn that God created the world in six days and rested on the seventh. Exodus 20:8-11 commands us to "remember Shabbat and keep it holy," while in Exodus 31:16-17, we read, "The people of Israel shall keep Shabbat, observing Shabbat throughout the generations as a covenant for all time. It shall be a sign for all time between Me and the people of Israel, for in six days God made heaven and earth, and on the seventh day God rested and was refreshed." Finally, in Deuteronomy 5:12-15, the second version of the Ten Commandments is given. At this point, as our people near the end of their wandering in the desert and are about to enter the Promised Land, we are told to "observe" Shabbat and keep it holy; we are given specific details for its observance; and we are reminded that we are obligated to do this because God led us out of Egypt, from slavery to freedom.

From slavery to freedom…. Only if one is free can one choose to set aside one day to rest and to remember, to keep and to observe Shabbat. Throughout the generations, in good times and bad, we Jews have observed Shabbat. For many poor people, Shabbat was the one bright spot in an otherwise bleak existence, the one time each week a man was a king and a woman was a queen, no matter how humble his or her surroundings. In each generation, Shabbat continues to remind us on a regular basis of our roots and of our covenant with God.

Home observance of Shabbat includes a Shabbat evening [Friday] dinner, made special in some way—perhaps by serving special foods and/or putting a fresh cloth or flowers on the table. Each family develops its own Shabbat traditions. (In my family, we always have peas. Why? My grandmother and mother always served peas on Shabbat, so that's one Shabbat "tradition" that has memories for us!) What's important is that you find traditions that will create Shabbat memories for you and your loved ones.

Lighting Shabbat candles is probably the most widely practiced Shabbat observance. It is first mentioned in biblical literature. We light two candles, which symbolize the two words *zachor*—remember—and—*shamor*—observe—that are mentioned in the two versions of the Ten Commandments. Both men and women can light Shabbat candles. The tradition is to light the candles first and then say the blessing.

When the candles are burning and Shabbat has officially begun, we say or chant the *Kiddush* over wine. While the first line of *Kiddush* is a blessing over wine, the rest is a blessing over Shabbat, sanctifying and setting it apart from the other days of the week.

After *Kiddush* we say or chant *Hamotzi*, the blessing over challah, which is a special twisted loaf of bread eaten by [many] Jews on Shabbat and other special occasions. While today we seek to eat breads that are full of healthy grains, in earlier times the white challah of Shabbat was a special treat compared to the darker and denser breads that were usually eaten during the week. The custom of having two loaves of challah reminds us of the double portion of manna that fell in the desert on Friday so that no Jew had to gather food on the seventh day, Shabbat. (A *midrash* tells us that a double portion that was gathered on any other day turned sour, but a double portion that was gathered on Friday remained fresh throughout Shabbat.)

Some Jewish parents also follow the lovely custom of blessing their children on Shabbat, with separate blessings for boys and girls.

If you have never celebrated Shabbat in your home, do not feel that you have to do everything at once. You may feel awkward at first, and you may feel discouraged. Choose to begin with one thing—candlelighting is what most people choose—and become comfortable with making that one observance a part of your tradition. Add other observances gradually.

I remember a line from an old song, "This is my once-a-year day." And I feel so lucky that in our tradition we have Shabbat—a "once-a-week day." Shabbat reminds us of the wonder of creation and gives us a weekly opportunity to "pause between the notes," to cherish our loved ones and our heritage. *Shabbat Shalom.*

Getting Ready

· · · · · · · · · ◆ · · · · · · · ·

The apparently simple idea that one day out of seven should be devoted to rest and reflection has always been a radical concept. Its earliest practice challenged the ancient world, where labor was the lot of beasts and slaves and leisure was the privilege of the rich and powerful. Today, when the hum of the machine never stops, when everyone has too much to do and not enough time in which to finish, Shabbat continues to pose fundamental questions about values and the value of life.

—ANITA DIAMANT AND HOWARD COOPER
LIVING A JEWISH LIFE

Preparing for Shabbat
A Frantic Approach

Joanne Doades

The dreams I have of careful, leisurely preparation for Shabbat never seem to become a reality. More often than not, during the frantic rush of getting my two small children ready for school on Friday morning, I remember that I haven't defrosted the meat for that evening and that our special Shabbat tablecloth was not taken to the cleaners after last Friday night.

How does a (part-time) businesswoman and (full-time) mother prepare for Shabbat? In a hurry! In our home, candles and kosher wine are considered staples, like bread and chocolate chip cookies. As soon as our supply begins to run low, we buy more, so that I never have to worry about those essentials at the last minute. Challah is purchased on Friday, posing a problem if we get to the bakery too late in the day. At our CLUWS [Come, Let Us Welcome Shabbat] workshop, I acquired the great idea of keeping a challah in the freezer for last-minute emergencies. That makes a lot of sense for a busy family like ours.

If I've forgotten to buy flowers for our Shabbat table, a hysterical late afternoon phone call to my husband always produces some. But now, as I sit here writing, I keep glancing at the beautiful tissue-paper flowers and the vase made from an orange juice can that my older daughter created at camp last summer and I wonder: Why didn't I ever think of using them?

If our special tablecloth has not been cleaned, I put on the next best one I have available. If we are not expecting company, I'm embarrassed to admit that I use our regular dishes, glasses, and utensils. I have neither the time nor the talent to cook gourmet meals, so unless we are having friends over, our Friday night meal is, I'm afraid, rather ordinary when judged by sophisticated culinary standards. What makes that event different in our home is that it is a meal: On all other nights, none of us (including me) knows what will end up on the table until the very last minute. But on Shabbat, we all know that I will somehow manage to come up with a dinner that will in some way be special for us.

At last, the moment arrives. My husband has miraculously managed to get home exactly when I had asked him to, and we have dragged the children, kicking and screaming, away from the TV set. We assemble around the candles. My little one lights first. She says the blessing for wine—*Baruch Atah Adonai Eloheinu Melech ha'olam borei peri hagafen*—instead of the blessing for candles. We do it together a second time: *Baruch Atah Adonai Eloheinu Melech ha'olam asher kideshanu bemitzvotav vetzivanu lehadlik ner shel Shabbat.*

My husband and I try saying the blessing for the children that I've just learned in the *Kabbalat Shabbat* workshop. We feel silly and uncomfortable. We try to look at them and touch them while reading our prayers. Impossible. I remind myself that giving birth isn't easy, either, but there's a good reason for doing it.

Finally, Ron and I turn to each other. "May God bless you and keep you," we say. My eyes fill with tears. I feel as though I'm seeing him for the very first time all week. How can this be? He is my husband. We share the most intimate joys and pains of life together. "May God look kindly upon you and be gracious to you." Why don't I see the love and tenderness in those eyes more often? Is he too busy supporting all of us, and am I too busy raising the children? "May God bestow favor upon you and give you peace." Could I consider him more in the week to come, let him know what a wonderful, tender husband and father he is? I put my arms around him and pray for the strength to be a more appreciative wife and a more patient mother in the days ahead. *Shabbat Shalom.*

Shabbat-On-Schedule: A Planning Guide

How can you make Shabbat a part of your life when you have never included it before?

Make Shabbat lists and charts on your computer. If you don't have a computer, copy the suggested lists and charts in this book. Post the lists on the refrigerator.

Just remember, nothing needs to be elaborate. If you can't cook, order in. Think about the special dish you might not make during the week or the special dessert you might add to the Shabbat menu. Consult Jewish cookbooks to see which foods are suggested. Keep the menu simple, but serve the same foods every Friday night to create a sense of continuity and ritual.

DAY/SUGGESTED ACTIVITY	YOUR NOTES	DATE
Sunday Invite guests?		
Monday Laundry for Shabbat?		

Tuesday
  Menu?
  Check supplies.
  • candles
  • wine/grape juice		

Wednesday
  Shop at supermarket/specialty
    stores. (Your weekly shopping list
    should include a Shabbat section.)
  Order by phone.
  Defrost if you are cooking on
    Thursday or Friday.		

Thursday
  Cook.
  Prepare to set or set table.		

Friday
  Buy/bake challah.
  Buy flowers.
  Tend to last-minute details.		

Items for a Festive Shabbat Table

Shabbat dinner is a time for celebration. You may be celebrating the fact that this is the only time during the hectic week you can sit down with your loved ones to share a meal. You may have arranged to have a dinner guest or to share a potluck supper. You may have decided to dine alone. You may be a college student who wants to spend some time with certain students or faculty. Getting ready for Shabbat is as simple or as complicated as you make it. You can be organized or spontaneous. In the beginning, we suggest that you keep your attempts simple.

Thinking ahead of time about how to celebrate Shabbat will help you reduce the stress of tackling this new experience. You will find it helpful to plan ahead and collect the following items for use on Friday night. Set aside a shelf or a drawer for these items so that they are available for speedy retrieval.

You Will Need	Alternatives
___ *Tzedakah* box	Substitute with any closed receptacle.
___ Candlesticks	
___ Matches	
___ Candles, preferably white	Substitute with any candles other than votive or memorial.
___ Wine/Grape juice	
___ Two loaves of challah	Substitute with two small braided rolls per person or two loaves of an unusual bread not used during the week.
___ Challah cover (preferably decorated with Shabbat motifs)	Substitute with a large paper/linen white napkin.

You May Opt For

___ Tablecloths or place mats, preferably white, to symbolize the Sabbath bride

___ Flowers or a plant as a table centerpiece

___ Tape recorder and tapes of Jewish, Israeli, and Shabbat music

According to the rabbinic principle of *hiddur mitzvah*, when a physical object is needed to fulfill a commandment, that object should be made as beautiful as possible. Thus, while it is perfectly acceptable to make a blessing over wine in a paper cup, it is even better to use a *Kiddush* cup, a beautiful goblet especially created for just that purpose. Over time, you may choose to purchase fancier items to use on Shabbat, such as an elaborate *Kiddush* cup or a pretty challah cover.

Shabbat Meal Reference Guide

In addition to recipes, many Jewish cookbooks contain wonderful commentary on Jewish customs and traditions. The Bibliography on pages 68–72 lists just a few cookbooks from the vast and interesting array that is available. Based on these books, we suggest the following foods for Friday night dinner.

Ashkenazic (Northern and Eastern European: Russia, Hungary, Poland, Germany, Austria, Lithuania)

Challah

Gefilte fish, horseradish

Chicken noodle/ matzah ball soup

Roast chicken or roast/potted meat

Kugel or knishes or kasha

Sweet dessert

Sephardic (Eastern Mediterranean, the Middle East, Caucasus and Central Asia, India, North Africa, the Maghreb)

Challah or *jachnoon* or *subya*— Sabbath bread with whole eggs

Marag—Yemenite bone soup

Samac—Yemenite fish—or *scheena*—Moroccan beef and potato roast—or Greek fish with plum sauce

Varied salads and pickled vegetables

Sweet dessert

Vegetarian

Challah
Mock chopped liver
Clear vegetable soup
Kneidlach—soup dumplings
Savory lentil and vegetable strudel
Carrot and potato tzimmes
Fasoulia
Roast potatoes or potato kugel
Cholemady—pickled vegetables

You may find it useful to make a few notes for future reference. Fill in the blanks on page 16 with the help of the yellow pages, friends, and Jewish acquaintances.

Weekly Shopping List

Wine/Grape juice _____   Flowers   _____

Challah   _____   Candles   _____

Local Supermarkets, Bakeries, Butchers That Carry Foods for Shabbat

Name of Store	Address/Phone	Name of Item(s)
_____	_____	_____
_____	_____	_____
_____	_____	_____

Take-out Services

Name	Address	Phone
_____	_____	_____
_____	_____	_____
_____	_____	_____

Cookbooks with Favorite or Appropriate Recipes

Name of Book	Recipe	Page
_____	_____	_____
_____	_____	_____
_____	_____	_____
_____	_____	_____
_____	_____	_____

Tasty Shabbat Recipes

Emergency Meat Loaf

> 2 pounds ground beef
> 3/4 cup bottled barbeque sauce
> 1/4 tsp. garlic salt
> 1/4 tsp. minced onion (optional)

Combine all ingredients. Form mixture into a loaf. Bake at 350°F. for 45 to 50 minutes. Serves 4-6.

Kibbutz Salad

> 3 large cucumbers, peeled and seeded
> 7 scallions
> 1 green pepper
> 2 tomatoes, pulp removed, diced
> 2 avocados, coarsely chopped
> 1 cup olives, pitted and chopped (or 2/3 cup nicoise olives left whole)
> 4 cloves garlic, mashed
> 2 tsps. kosher salt
> 1 tsp. freshly ground pepper
> 1/2 tsp. cumin
> 1/3 cup olive oil
> juice of 1 lemon

Prepare the vegetables and put them into a bowl. Mash the garlic with a fork and combine with the powdered spices. Slowly add the olive oil and then the lemon juice. Mix constantly. Pour the mixture over the vegetables.

—ALAYNE ZATULOVE

Klops I

(SAVORY CASSEROLE)

> 1 cup brown lentils, soaked overnight and rinsed well
> 2 1/2 cups water *or* vegetable stock
> 2 medium onions, sliced
> 2 cloves garlic, crushed/minced
> 1 medium carrot, grated/shredded

2 tbsps. corn oil

1 cup mushrooms, chopped

1 tsp. yeast extract or soy sauce

1 tbsp. tomato puree/paste

1 tbsp. chopped parsley

2 tbsps. wheat germ

1/4 cup vegetable stock

sea salt and freshly ground black pepper

chili powder *or* cayenne pepper

1 tbsp. lemon juice

1/4 cup cheese grated/shredded

1 cup fresh whole wheat breadcrumbs

Bring the soaked lentils to a boil in the water or vegetable stock and simmer until they are tender (about 30 minutes). Sauté the onions, garlic, and carrot in the oil until they are softened (about 15 minutes). Add the mushrooms and cook for 10 more minutes. Preheat the oven to 375°F.

Mash the cooked lentils with a potato/vegetable masher or puree them in a liquidizer or food processor. The mixture should not be too smooth. Combine the lentil puree, the onion-garlic-carrot-mushroom mixture, and the remaining ingredients together well, except for the lemon juice, cheese, and breadcrumbs. Spoon the mixture into a well-greased casserole dish and sprinkle the lemon juice over it. Bake in the preheated oven for about 45 minutes. Sprinkle the cheese and breadcrumbs on the top about 20 minutes before the end of the cooking time.

Klops II

(SAVORY CASSEROLE)

1 cup mixed nuts, finely chopped (cashews, hazelnuts/filberts, walnuts)

1 large onion, finely grated/shredded

1/2 cup fresh whole wheat breadcrumbs

2 free-range eggs

1 tbsp. fresh parsley

1 tbsp. yeast extract *or* soy sauce

sea salt and freshly ground pepper

2 cups tomato juice

Preheat the oven to 350°F. Put all the ingredients except the tomato juice into a bowl and mix together well. Spoon the mixture into a greased casserole dish and pour the tomato juice on the top. Bake in the preheated oven for 45-60 minutes. (Cover the casserole halfway through if it seems to be drying out.) Serve with brown rice, vegetables, or salads.

Note: You can decorate this dish by lining the bottom and sides of the casserole dish with onion rings, zucchini slices, and celery sticks before you put the mixture into the casserole. A topping can be made by sautéing finely chopped or pureed mushrooms with finely chopped or pureed onion and spreading this mixture over the Klops mixture before you bake it in the oven.

—ROSE FRIEDMAN, *JEWISH VEGETARIAN COOKING*

Curried Rice with Nuts

(TRADITIONAL FOR JEWS OF INDIA)

> 4 cups water
> salt
> 1 tsp. saffron
> 1 tsp. curry powder
> 2 cups rice
> 2/3 cup seedless raisins
> 1/4 cup oil for frying
> 3 ozs. walnuts, chopped

In a saucepan, bring the water, salt, saffron, and curry powder to a boil. Rinse the rice thoroughly, add it to the saucepan, and cook the mixture for 10–15 minutes, until it is tender. Skim the foam forming on the top so that the rice remains clear. Remove the mixture from the heat and drain. Put the mixture into a bowl and set aside. Rinse the raisins in water. Heat the oil in a pan, sauté the nuts, and remove them from the oil. Sauté the raisins in the oil until they are brownish. Remove the raisins and pour a little of the heated oil over the rice. Garnish the rice with the fried nuts and raisins. Serve as a main dish or second course, with no side dishes.

—ALDO NAHOUM, *THE ART OF ISRAELI COOKING*

Shabbat Dinner Shopping List

Shabbat dinner on _____

Food	Purchased at	Phone
_____	_____	_____
_____	_____	_____
_____	_____	_____
_____	_____	_____
_____	_____	_____
_____	_____	_____
_____	_____	_____
_____	_____	_____
_____	_____	_____

Ritual Items	Store/Phone
Wine: Brand/type/size _____	_____
Grape juice: Brand/type/size _____	_____
Challah _____	_____
Candles _____	_____
Centerpiece _____	_____

Resources for Jewish Ritual Observance Items

Shabbat candles: Stocked by most supermarkets in the kosher section; some Judaica bookstores have a supply or can direct you to a manufacturer or distributor.

Challah: Jewish or German bakeries, the frozen food case of most supermarkets, cookbooks (see Bibliography, page 69).

Wine: Many wine/liquor stores carry kosher wine.

Grape juice (white/red): Supermarkets.

All other items: Temple gift shops, Judaica stores, mail-order houses that sell Judaica, *yahrzeit* (memorial) candles. See Shabbat candles, above.

Shabbat Menu/Shopping List

Butcher _____

My Favorite Take-out Service(s)

Item	Store and Address	Phone
_____	_____	_____
_____	_____	_____
_____	_____	_____
_____	_____	_____
_____	_____	_____
_____	_____	_____
_____	_____	_____
_____	_____	_____

What guests can bring:_____

_____

_____

Welcoming Shabbat

• • • • • • • • • • ◆ • • • • • • • •

[Shabbat] is a weekly respite from endless toil and competition. Interrupting the pursuit of wealth and power, it turns the Jew toward the meaning of human existence. Given a day without labor, the individual can concentrate on being a creature fashioned in the divine image. On Shabbat we take delight in the beauty of creation, spending time with family, friends, and community and recharging our physical and spiritual batteries for the week ahead.

—Peter S. Knobel, ed.
Gates of the Seasons
A Guide to the Jewish Year

A Suggested Order for Welcoming Shabbat at Home

There are many ways to welcome Shabbat. At the end of the sixteenth century, the Kabbalists who lived in Safed, a city in northern Israel, welcomed Shabbat in a special way. On Friday afternoon, they would dress in white and walk to the gates of the city to greet their weekly guest—the Sabbath bride. As they walked, they would chant, *Lecha dodi likrat kalah penei Shabbat nekabalah*—"Let us go and greet the Sabbath bride."

To prepare for *Kabbalat Shabbat*, arrange the meal and set the table in a way that establishes a festive environment, one that reflects the Jewish people's "romance with the Sabbath bride." As you go through each step of *Kabbalat Shabbat*, refer to "Blessings for Shabbat" on pages 37–40 to help you gain a greater facility with the Shabbat prayers and rituals. As you become more familiar with the process of welcoming Shabbat, you will develop your own rituals. In the meantime, here is an informal guide.

1. Give *tzedakah* to remind us that God created the world and that we, as God's partners, are responsible for maintaining it. We can choose to give time and/or worldly goods. On Friday evening, we put money into a *tzedakah* box to help those who are in need.

2. Say *Shehecheyanu*. At your first Shabbat meal, you might choose to recite this blessing that celebrates any new experience in one's life.

3. Light candles and recite the blessing—*Hadlakat Nerot*. The candles remind us of creation, when light followed darkness. The two white candles symbolize God's commandments to remember—*zachor*—and observe—*shamor*—the Sabbath. (Optional: Follow with a wish for *Shabbat Shalom* and hugs, kisses, and handshakes.)

4. Bless our children, each other, and/or a movement or a cause. Based on the Torah, we invoke God's blessing for our loved ones.

5. Say/sing *Kiddush*, the blessing over wine and the blessing that sanctifies the Sabbath. We use wine as our symbol of joy, and we bless God as the Creator of the fruit of the vine. (At this point, we do not drink but continue the prayer.) Then we thank God for giving us Shabbat as a reminder to cherish all forms of creation and freedom. (At this point, we may drink.)

6. Pour water over our hands as the ancient priests did before making sacrifices and say the blessing—*Netilat Yadayim.*

7. Say/sing *Hamotzi,* the blessing over challah, to thank God for providing food from the earth. We then cut or tear the challah and salt our piece. We use two loaves of challah as a remembrance of the double portion of manna that God provided for the Children of Israel on Shabbat.

8. Eat the Shabbat meal, *se'udat Shabbat.* This is a festive dinner at which the business of the week should not be discussed. Conversation should center on family, friends, and the environment (nonmaterial, noncompetitive); celebrations (birthdays, anniversaries); good experiences of the past week; our Jewish heritage; and ideas for the repair of the world.

9. Sing *zemirot.* These Shabbat songs can be sung before, during, and after the meal.

10. Give thanks for the meal by saying/singing *Birkat Hamazon.* You might choose to create your own grace after meals.

Clues about Shabbat
Questions and Answers

These topics follow the recommended order for welcoming Shabbat at home.

Tzedakah

Tzedakah comes from the Hebrew word *tzedek*, which means "justice" or "righteousness." It is often used to mean "charity" or "charitable acts." The word *charity* is derived from the Latin *carus*, meaning "dearness" or "love." The implication of this combination of translations is that if we desire to live a life that is just and righteous, we must share our worldly possessions.

Tzedakah must be given with sympathy and good grace, so that the dignity of the recipient is not reduced. Poor people as well as wealthy individuals are required to give charity, if not in money or food, then in kindness of heart and good deeds.

Moses Maimonides (1135-1204 C.E.) discusses *tzedakah* in the seventh book of the *Mishneh Torah*, a compendium of the laws of the Torah. He lists the eight degrees of giving *tzedakah*, each one higher than the next:

- To give grudgingly, reluctantly, or with regret.
- To give less than one should but with grace.
- To give what one should but only after being asked.
- To give before one is asked.
- To give without knowing who the receiver will be, although the latter knows the identity of the giver.
- To give without making one's identity known.
- To give so that neither the giver nor the receiver knows each other's identity.
- To help another become self-supporting by means of a gift or loan or by finding employment for the one in need.

1. What is *tzedakah*?

    Tzedakah is a charitable act through which one individual enables another to fulfill his/her potential. It can include the giving of time—

gemilut chasadim—and/or possessions for the benefit of others.

2. How is *tzedakah* money collected?

A *tzedakah* box, which is similar to a piggy bank, is frequently used. A *tzedakah* box can be obtained from an established organization that collects funds for a particular cause, can be purchased at a store, or can be homemade.

3. What is significant about the connection between *tzedakah* and *Kabbalat Shabbat*?

Shabbat recognizes the centrality of liberating the oppressed. *Tzedakah* is a meaningful expression of this concern.

4. Is the cause or recipient preselected?

Sometimes the *tzedakah* box is specially marked. If an unmarked box is used, all the members of the household can discuss the needs that exist in their community and can decide together where the money should go once the box is full.

5. How can we remind ourselves about the special relationship between *tzedakah* and Shabbat?

Keep your *tzedakah* box together with your Shabbat candlesticks in a visible place in the living/dining area as a constant reminder that Shabbat is coming. *Tzedakah* is given prior to the lighting of candles.

Candlelighting

(For blessing, see page 37.)

Although the lighting of candles is a ritual universally performed among Jews, no injunction to light candles—even Shabbat candles—appears in the Bible. Some rabbis and scholars believe that the lighting of candles began as a custom to symbolize the biblical injunction that the Jews "shall be a light to the nations." More pragmatic thinkers believe that the lighting of candles— which contributed a sense of warmth and illumination in an age that did not have electricity—provided a logical and practical way to make the Sabbath a special time in the home.

1. Do I need particular candlesticks for Shabbat?

    Just as we set aside time for the ritual of candlelighting, you may choose to set aside certain candlesticks to be used only on Shabbat.

2. How many candles should be lit?

    At least two candles are kindled as symbols of the two biblical phrases "Remember the Sabbath day" and "Observe the Sabbath day." Some families light an additional candle for each child. In other families, every person at the table has a set of favorite candlesticks. Some people include a candle for parents or grandparents who have died.

3. When are candles lit?

    In many homes, Jews light candles eighteen to twenty minutes before sunset on Friday. In others, candlelighting takes place when all the participants are present to begin *Kabbalat Shabbat*.

4. Can one Shabbat candle be used to light another?

    Once lit, a Shabbat candle becomes a symbol of the restful beauty experienced during Shabbat. Try not to put a Shabbat candle "to work." Provide an extra candle or matches to ignite the remaining wicks.

5. Who lights the candles?

    Customarily, women light the Shabbat candles, after which they cover their eyes and recite the blessing. According to Maimonides, since women are usually at home preparing for the Sabbath at the moment of candlelighting, this responsibility should be theirs. Men, however, are not exempt from candlelighting responsibilities. Should a woman not dwell in the home or be absent from it at the time of candlelighting, the man is obliged to light the candles and say the blessing. Many Jews prefer an egalitarian approach to all rituals, in which case, everyone regardless of age or gender is encouraged to light candles and recite the blessing together.

6. Should both men and women wear head coverings to light candles?
   Family traditions differ.

7. Can I move or blow out Shabbat candles?
   If we are to enjoy the beauty of the glow of the Shabbat lights well into the evening, Shabbat candles should be allowed to extinguish themselves. You may take safety precautions by placing the candles on a tray covered with tinfoil or in a shallow pan of water.

8. Is there any particular order to be used for lighting the Shabbat candles during Chanukah?
   Light the Chanukah holiday candles first and then light the Shabbat candles.

9. Can I recite special prayers after the candlelighting prayer?
   Candlelighting is a wonderful time for private meditation because by lighting candles, you have framed yourself in sacred time. In some homes, the father and children extol the mother by singing or reciting *Eshet Chayil*—"A Woman of Valor." (Proverbs 31:10-31)

The Blessing of Children

(For blessings, see page 37.)

Parental blessing of children is first found in Genesis 27:1–29:9. In *The Torah: A Modern Commentary*, Rabbi Plaut states, "Such a blessing was accorded special significance…. The parent appeared to be in God's stead, and while he had no power to bind the Divinity he invoked, his words were believed to reflect prophetic vision." Because God blessed Isaac after Abraham died (Genesis 25:11), Isaac was enabled to bless the next generation. So, too, we as parents continue the tradition from generation to generation.

1. When are blessings of children conferred?

    Blessings of children are considered so important that traditionally they are conferred immediately after the Shabbat candles are lit. The celebration of Shabbat is the celebration of creation (Genesis) and freedom (Exodus). By blessing our children, we are acknowledging that from generation to generation, we are fulfilling and perpetuating creation and God's will.

2. Who confers the blessings?

    In a traditional household, it is the father who blesses the children. In other households, the blessings are conferred by the father and/or the mother. In some families, anyone who wishes to bless family and friends can do so.

3. What does the person who is conferring the blessings say?

    Ideally, the person says an individual prayer for each child. However, other prayers can be added. The traditional blessing refers to Ephraim and Manasseh, the sons of the biblical patriarch Joseph, as well as to the four matriarchs. The names of our ancestors are followed by the priestly blessings found in Numbers 6:24–26.

4. What does the person who is conferring the blessings do?

    The person places both hands on the top of each child's bowed head or shoulders and pronounces the blessing.

Note: Some spouses may also choose to bless each other. In some families, all who are present bless one another.

Kiddush

(For blessings, see page 38.)

Kiddush means "sanctification." It is a proclamation of the holiness of the day or festival and is recited over a cup of wine on the eve of the Sabbath and the festivals.

Kiddush tells of God's completion of the world on the seventh day and God's blessing of that day, calling it holy because God's work was done; it contains praise and thanks to God for creating the fruit of the vine, a symbol of joy; and it notes that remembering and observing the Sabbath is a commandment given in love by God to commemorate creation and the Exodus from Egypt.

1. Why do we use wine for *Kiddush*?

   Kiddush is the prayer that is recited or chanted to sanctify the Sabbath and the festival day. Wine is a symbol of joy and life. For Jews, *Kiddush* is the "ritual salute" at joyous occasions.

2. Can any wines be used?

   Suit your taste. Sweet wine is associated with a sweet Shabbat, but you may use any wine. Some suggest that a particular brand in a special decanter be set aside for Shabbat. Many choose a kosher wine since blessings are recited over it.

3. Are there substitutes for wine?

   Use grape juice or any beverage produced from the fruit of the vine.

4. How many *Kiddush* cups or wine glasses are used?

   Customs vary. Some families use one large *Kiddush* cup and pass it around after the prayer has been recited. Others use a cup for each person. In some families, wine is poured from the one large *Kiddush* cup into individual cups after the prayer has been recited.

5. Who recites or sings *Kiddush*?

   In some homes, one person recites or sings *Kiddush*. In other households, there are choices: singing in unison, rotating leaders, etc.

6. Do we sit or stand when reciting/singing *Kiddush*?

   Do whatever makes this essential prayer special for you.

Hamotzi

(For blessing, see page 38.)

The literal translation of *hamotzi* is "who brings forth." When we "break bread," we praise God for bringing forth grains from the earth.

Before the destruction of the Second Temple in 70 C.E., freshly baked breads were brought to the Temple and placed by the priests on a table in the sanctuary of the Tabernacle on Shabbat.

After the destruction of the Second Temple, ritual observance was decentralized and Shabbat began to be observed in the home. The dining table became the equivalent of the altar, and challah, covered by a beautiful cloth cover, came to symbolize the altar offering.

1. What is the significance of the word *hamotzi*?

    The word *hamotzi* denotes God's role as the source of our sustenance. Bread is used as the symbol of food when we recite or chant the *berachah*—"blessing"—that includes the word *hamotzi*. The blessing emphasizes the partnership between God and humanity because while God has created the ingredients that are in bread, we must collect them and complete the process of making the bread.

2. What kind of bread is used on Shabbat?

    People of Eastern European heritage use challah, an oblong braided bread. Sephardim—the Jews of Southern Europe, North Africa, and the Middle East—use a wide variety of breads indigenous to their culture. To welcome the Sabbath, most Jews use two loaves of breads (see page 24).

3. What do I do with the loaves?

    There are many customs connected with blessing the Sabbath breads:
    - The loaves are covered prior to the recital of the blessing.
    - One person holds the uncovered breads, flat sides together, for all to see as the blessing is recited.
    - Everyone at the table touches the uncovered breads and recites the blessing together.
    - After the blessing for bread has been recited, the loaves are cut or torn and the pieces are passed around the table.

Shabbat Miscellany

1. When does Shabbat start?

   Individuals' own religious response determines when they begin their celebration of Shabbat. Some Jews check calendars, Jewish weeklies, and even the front page of Friday's *New York Times* for the time of sunset on Friday evening. They light candles eighteen minutes before sunset and consider Shabbat to have begun at that time. Other Jews begin Shabbat after they have returned from synagogue and have finished their preparations.

2. What should I wear on Shabbat?

   Some people make an effort not only to clean and prepare their home for the arrival of Shabbat but also to dress up. Traditionally, we greet Shabbat as a long-awaited guest. Many families put on their Shabbat clothes (festive clothing) to greet the Sabbath bride. Other families prefer to wear their most comfortable clothing.

3. Do other people have to be with me to welcome Shabbat at home?

   No. But keep in mind that Shabbat is an opportunity for togetherness, a time for family members and friends to connect. Whether a family consists of single individuals, friends, varied groupings of grandparents, parents, children, and relatives, spouses, partners, or the "congregational family," it is considered a *mitzvah* to share the Shabbat meal with others.

4. Is it possible to get home in time, complete the ritual, put dinner on the table, carry on a conversation, clear, clean, attend temple on time, and still start to slow down?

   The answer is yes. Begin by choosing just a few practices from this book that appeal to you. Each week or month, you can add a few more. As you become accustomed to setting aside time to make Shabbat, you may discover that performing a few rituals thoroughly and at a relaxed pace is more rewarding than rushing to do many things carelessly. For example, you may find that allowing more time to linger at the Shabbat dinner table results in a richer, more nourishing experience for body and soul. Through experimentation and trial and error, you will eventually develop your own routine.

5. Can I celebrate Shabbat if I am traveling?

   Shabbat can be welcomed in hotel rooms, campsites, anywhere. Improvisation can add a special quality to *Kabbalat Shabbat*. Use fresh grapes, regional bread, a thermos for wine/grape juice, collapsible cups, matches, candles placed in an ashtray or on a tray covered with tinfoil or into impromptu candle holders made of empty soda cans. Remember: Shabbat is a state of mind as well as a set of rituals.

6. What should I expect if I am invited to celebrate Shabbat in a traditionally observant home?

Individuals who follow *halachah*—rabbinic law—celebrate Shabbat with the same items, sing the same songs, and recite the same blessings as you will find in this book. If you celebrate Shabbat in an Orthodox home, you will notice that all the electrical appliances have been turned off, kept on for the duration of Shabbat, or put on a timer. No work as defined by the rabbis is done in such a home on Shabbat. Work, according to *halachah*, includes any action that was used to build the Temple in Jerusalem. Thirty-nine categories of labor are defined in the Talmud. They include activities such as sewing, writing, shaving, baking, playing musical instruments, and other forms of creating. In an Orthodox home, Shabbat candles are lit eighteen minutes before sunset and are not moved after they have been lit. Only kosher wine is used for *Kiddush*. Before *Hamotzi* is recited, it is customary for individuals to wash their hands and say a blessing. No words are spoken between the time of washing and the recitation of *Hamotzi*. After that blessing has been recited/sung, the *challot* are sliced and the pieces are passed around the table. Males wear *kippot*—head coverings—at the table. When an individual recites a prayer, the others respond by saying Amen. The person reciting the prayer does not say Amen at the end of his or her own blessing.

The meal consists of kosher food. No shellfish or pork products are eaten, the meat has been ritually slaughtered, and milk and meat products are not served at the same meal. After dinner, *zemirot* are sung and *Birkat Hamazon* is recited.

7. What if I make a mistake?

The word *mistake* is not part of the *Kabbalat Shabbat* vocabulary. The only mistake you can make is not trying.

The Shabbat Meal

1. Should there be a special menu for Shabbat dinner?

    Yes. The menu should reflect the festivity and uniqueness of Friday night. Many people enjoy particular foods considered traditional for the Sabbath. Favorite foods not served during the week could be served on Friday evening. If you have no time to cook or bake, choose from the array of prepared foods available in the frozen food section of your supermarket or from take-out stores.

2. Why should the Shabbat meal be special?

    The meal enhances the celebration. Some suggest that the meal helps the body and soul find fulfillment—*shalom*. Gloria Silverman, a full-time working mother of two teenagers, sets aside Thursday night for Shabbat preparation. She cooks and sets her table, using her best china and tableware. She puts her Shabbat candles in their holders. When she stops to pick up her *challot,* she also buys a favorite cake that is eaten only on Friday night, since the family "diets during the week."

Zemirot

1. What are *zemirot*?

   Zemirot are songs, poems, and hymns about Shabbat. They can be sung in Hebrew, Yiddish, or a native language. They can be chanted at the beginning of the *Kabbalat Shabbat* ritual, at any time during the Friday night meal, and/or at its end. They can also be sung during other Sabbath meals.

2. How do *zemirot* differ from other table songs?

   In most other cultures, table songs are drinking songs. *Zemirot* are songs of thanks.

3. How can we introduce *zemirot* in a relaxed, noncontrived way?

   Start with one easy song. Make sure that everyone has a copy. Initially sing that song every Friday evening. Then begin adding more songs to your repertoire.

Birkat Hamazon

(FOR GRACE AFTER MEALS, SEE PAGE 38.)

1. Who recites *Birkat Hamazon*?

   Customarily, the leader invites those present to join in the blessings. Everyone responds, chanting in unison.

2. When is *Birkat Hamazon* recited?

   Traditionally, it is said after every meal. Reciting *Birkat Hamazon* is sufficient, but anyone present can offer an additional prayer.

3. Is the Shabbat *Birkat Hamazon* different from the *Birkat Hamazon* that is recited on other days?

   On Shabbat, festivals, and joyous occasions, Psalm 126, "A Pilgrim Song," is sung as an introduction. On Shabbat a special prayer for peace is added. In it we ask God for an inheritance of a Shabbat of eternal peace.

Blessings for Shabbat

THE ACCOMPANYING COMPACT DISK WILL ASSIST YOU IN LEARNING THE MUSIC AND
WORDS OF THE FOLLOWING BLESSINGS, AS WELL AS SEVERAL TRADITIONAL AND CONTEM-
PORARY SHABBAT COMPOSITIONS.

Shehecheyanu (upon celebrating one's first Shabbat)

בָּרוּךְ אַתָּה יְיָ אֱלֹהֵינוּ מֶלֶךְ הָעוֹלָם שֶׁהֶחֱיָנוּ וְקִיְּמָנוּ וְהִגִּיעָנוּ לַזְּמַן הַזֶּה.

*Baruch Atah Adonai Eloheinu Melech ha'olam shehecheyanu vekiyemanu
vehigianu lazeman hazeh.*

Blessed are You, *Adonai* our God, Ruler of the universe, for giving us life, for
sustaining us, and for enabling us to reach this time.

Candlelighting

בָּרוּךְ אַתָּה יְיָ אֱלֹהֵינוּ מֶלֶךְ הָעוֹלָם אֲשֶׁר קִדְּשָׁנוּ בְּמִצְוֹתָיו וְצִוָּנוּ
לְהַדְלִיק נֵר שֶׁל שַׁבָּת.

*Baruch Atah Adonai Eloheinu Melech ha'olam asher kideshanu bemitzvotav
vetzivanu lehadlik ner shel Shabbat.*

Blessed are You, *Adonai* our God, Ruler of the universe, who has made us
holy with commandments and commanded us to kindle the lights of Shabbat.

The Blessing of Children

יְשִׂמְךָ אֱלֹהִים כְּאֶפְרַיִם וְכִמְנַשֶּׁה.

Yesimcha Elohim ke-Efrayim vechi-Menasheh.

May God inspire you to live in the tradition of Ephraim and Manasseh.

יְשִׂמֵךְ אֱלֹהִים כְּשָׂרָה רִבְקָה רָחֵל וְלֵאָה.

Yesimech Elohim ke-Sarah Rivkah Rachel ve-Leah.

May God inspire you to live in the tradition of Sarah, Rebecca, Rachel, and
Leah.

יְבָרֶכְךָ יְיָ וְיִשְׁמְרֶךָ. יָאֵר יְיָ פָּנָיו אֵלֶיךָ וִיחֻנֶּךָ. יִשָּׂא יְיָ פָּנָיו אֵלֶיךָ
וְיָשֵׂם לְךָ שָׁלוֹם.

*Yevarechecha Adonai veyishmerecha. Ya'er Adonai panav elecha vichuneka.
Yisa Adonai panav elecha veyasem lecha shalom.*

May God bless you and keep you. May God look kindly upon you and be gracious to you. May God bestow favor upon you and grant you peace.

Kiddush (abbreviated version)

בָּרוּךְ אַתָּה יְיָ אֱלֹהֵינוּ מֶלֶךְ הָעוֹלָם בּוֹרֵא פְּרִי הַגָּפֶן.

Baruch Atah Adonai Eloheinu Melech ha'olam borei peri hagafen.

Blessed are You, *Adonai* our God, Ruler of the universe, Creator of the fruit of the vine.

בָּרוּךְ אַתָּה יְיָ אֱלֹהֵינוּ מֶלֶךְ הָעוֹלָם מְקַדֵּשׁ הַשַּׁבָּת.

Baruch Atah Adonai Eloheinu Melech ha'olam mekadesh ha-Shabbat.

Blessed are You, *Adonai* our God, who hallows the Shabbat.

Hamotzi

בָּרוּךְ אַתָּה יְיָ אֱלֹהֵינוּ מֶלֶךְ הָעוֹלָם הַמּוֹצִיא לֶחֶם מִן הָאָרֶץ.

Baruch Atah Adonai Eloheinu Melech ha'olam hamotzi lechem min ha'aretz.

Blessed are You, *Adonai* our God, Ruler of the universe, who brings forth bread from the earth.

Birkat Hamazon

A PILGRIM SONG

שִׁיר הַמַּעֲלוֹת

בְּשׁוּב יְיָ אֶת־שִׁיבַת צִיּוֹן הָיִינוּ כְּחֹלְמִים. אָז יִמָּלֵא שְׂחוֹק פִּינוּ וּלְשׁוֹנֵנוּ רִנָּה. אָז יֹאמְרוּ בַגּוֹיִם הִגְדִּיל יְיָ לַעֲשׂוֹת עִם־אֵלֶּה. הִגְדִּיל יְיָ לַעֲשׂוֹת עִמָּנוּ הָיִינוּ שְׂמֵחִים. שׁוּבָה יְיָ אֶת־שְׁבִיתֵנוּ כַּאֲפִיקִים בַּנֶּגֶב. הַזֹּרְעִים בְּדִמְעָה בְּרִנָּה יִקְצֹרוּ. הָלוֹךְ יֵלֵךְ וּבָכֹה נֹשֵׂא מֶשֶׁךְ־הַזָּרַע בֹּא־יָבוֹא בְרִנָּה נֹשֵׂא אֲלֻמֹּתָיו.

Shir hama'alot beshuv Adonai et shivat Tziyon hayinu kecholmim. Az yimale sechok pinu uleshonenu rinah. Az yomru vagoyim higdil Adonai la' asot im eleh. Higdil Adonai la'asot imanu hayinu semechim. Shuvah Adonai et shevitenu ka'afikim banegev. Hazorim bedimah berinah yiktzoru. Haloch yelech uvacho nosei meshech hazara bo yavo verinah nosei alumotav.

When God brought back the exiles to Zion, we were like those who dream. Then our mouths were filled with laughter, our tongues with joyful song. Then they said among the nations: "God has done great things for them." Yes,

God has done great things for us, and we rejoiced. Restore our exiles, O God, as streams revive the desert. They who sow in tears shall reap in joy. Although he goes forth weeping, carrying the measure of the seed, he shall come home in joy, bearing his sheaves.

LEADER

חֲבֵרַי נְבָרֵךְ.

Chaverai nevarech.

Friends, let us say grace.

RESPONSE

יְהִי שֵׁם יְיָ מְבֹרָךְ מֵעַתָּה וְעַד עוֹלָם.

Yehi shem Adonai mevorach me'atah ve'ad olam.

May God's name be blessed now and forever.

LEADER

יְהִי שֵׁם יְיָ מְבֹרָךְ מֵעַתָּה וְעַד עוֹלָם. בִּרְשׁוּת חֲבֵרַי נְבָרֵךְ (אֱלֹהֵינוּ)*
שֶׁאָכַלְנוּ מִשֶּׁלּוֹ.

Yehi shem Adonai mevorach me'atah ve'ad olam. Birshut chaverai nevarech (Eloheinu) she'achalnu mishelo.*

May God's name be blessed now and forever. Let us bless our God of whose bounty we have partaken.

RESPONSE

בָּרוּךְ (אֱלֹהֵינוּ)* שֶׁאָכַלְנוּ מִשֶּׁלּוֹ וּבְטוּבוֹ חָיִינוּ.

Baruch (Eloheinu) she'achalnu mishelo uvetuvo chayinu.*

Blessed be our God of whose bounty we have partaken and through whose goodness we live.

LEADER

בָּרוּךְ (אֱלֹהֵינוּ)* שֶׁאָכַלְנוּ מִשֶּׁלּוֹ וּבְטוּבוֹ חָיִינוּ. בָּרוּךְ הוּא וּבָרוּךְ שְׁמוֹ.

Baruch (Eloheinu) she'achalnu mishelo uvetuvo chayinu. Baruch hu uvaruch shemo.*

Blessed be our God of whose bounty we have partaken and through whose goodness we live. Blessed be God and blessed be God's name.

---

* Said when ten or more are present at the meal.

בָּרוּךְ אַתָּה יְיָ אֱלֹהֵינוּ מֶלֶךְ הָעוֹלָם הַזָּן אֶת הָעוֹלָם כֻּלוֹ בְּטוּבוֹ בְּחֵן
בְּחֶסֶד וּבְרַחֲמִים. הוּא נוֹתֵן לֶחֶם לְכָל בָּשָׂר כִּי לְעוֹלָם חַסְדּוֹ. וּבְטוּבוֹ
הַגָּדוֹל תָּמִיד לֹא חָסַר לָנוּ וְאַל יֶחְסַר לָנוּ מָזוֹן לְעוֹלָם וָעֶד בַּעֲבוּר שְׁמוֹ
הַגָּדוֹל. כִּי הוּא אֵל זָן וּמְפַרְנֵס לַכֹּל וּמֵטִיב לַכֹּל וּמֵכִין מָזוֹן לְכָל־
בְּרִיּוֹתָיו אֲשֶׁר בָּרָא. בָּרוּךְ אַתָּה יְיָ הַזָּן אֶת־הַכֹּל.

*Baruch Atah Adonai Eloheinu Melech ha'olam hazan et ha'olam kulo betuvo
bechen bechesed uverachamim. Hu noten lechem lechol basar ki le'olam chasdo.
Uvetuvo hagadol tamid lo chasar lanu ve'al yechsar lanu mazon le'olam va'ed
ba'avur shemo hagadol. Ki hu El zan umefarnes lakol umetiv lakol umechin
mazon lechol beriyotav asher bara. Baruch Atah Adonai hazan et hakol.*

Blessed are You, *Adonai* our God, Ruler of the universe, who sustains the
whole world with goodness, with grace, with kindness, and with tender
mercy. God gives food to every creature, for God's kindness endures forever.
Through God's great goodness, food has never failed us, and may it not fail us
forever and ever, for God's great name's sake. For God nourishes and sustains
all and does good unto all, providing food for all the creatures whom God has
fashioned. Blessed are You, *Adonai*, who gives food to all.

וּבְנֵה יְרוּשָׁלַיִם עִיר הַקֹּדֶשׁ בִּמְהֵרָה בְיָמֵינוּ. בָּרוּךְ אַתָּה יְיָ בּוֹנֵה
בְרַחֲמָיו יְרוּשָׁלָיִם. אָמֵן.

*Uveneh Yerushalayim ir hakodesh bimherah beyamenu. Baruch Atah
Adonai boneh verachamav Yerushalayim. Amen.*

And build Jerusalem as a holy city speedily in our time. Blessed are You,
Adonai, who in mercy builds Jerusalem.

הָרַחֲמָן הוּא יַנְחִילֵנוּ יוֹם שֶׁכֻּלוֹ שַׁבָּת.

Harachaman hu yanchilenu yom shekulo Shabbat.

Merciful One, help us to see the coming of a time that is all Shabbat.

עֹשֶׂה שָׁלוֹם בִּמְרוֹמָיו הוּא יַעֲשֶׂה שָׁלוֹם עָלֵינוּ וְעַל־כָּל־יִשְׂרָאֵל וְאִמְרוּ אָמֵן.

*Oseh shalom bimromav hu ya'aseh shalom aleinu ve'al kol Yisrael ve'imru
amen.*

May the Source of perfect peace grant peace to us, to all Israel, and to all the
world, and let us say Amen.

יְיָ עֹז לְעַמּוֹ יִתֵּן יְיָ יְבָרֵךְ אֶת־עַמּוֹ בַשָּׁלוֹם.

Adonai oz le'amo yiten Adonai yevarech et amo vashalom.

Adonai will give strength to God's people. *Adonai* will bless God's people
with peace.

Shabbat Enrichment

· · · · · · · · · · ◆ · · · · · · · · ·

As a reminder of creation, Shabbat affords us a singular opportunity to reflect on the marvel of the universe and to contemplate our part in the continuing process of life.

—PETER S. KNOBEL, ED.
GATES OF THE SEASONS
A GUIDE TO THE JEWISH YEAR

Torah Study: Talmud Torah

According to talmudic tradition, a portion of the Torah, called a *parashah* or *sidrah*, is read publicly on Shabbat, Monday, Thursday, and holidays so that the Jewish people never have to go longer than three days without hearing the Torah.

Today, our public Torah readings take place during worship services and our Torah study begins with the accompanying sermon, but our opportunities for study go far beyond weekly services. *Talmud Torah*—the *mitzvah* of Torah study—says that we should study Torah every day and especially on Shabbat. The synagogue is sometimes called *beit midrash*—"house of study"—because of the many opportunities for study that exist within its walls, ranging from study groups to lecture series, from religious school to adult education.

But Torah study need not be confined to the synagogue. You can study alone at home. Some people find partners with whom they study regularly. Others prefer to form a study group or to join an existing group with a discussion leader, often sponsored by a congregation. The traditionally observant spend Shabbat afternoon studying the weekly *parashah*, along with other works or commentaries. Regardless of the format you choose, you may find it helpful to begin your studies by following this brief guide.

Steps to Studying Torah

1. Read the entire *parashah*. Establish a context for the text by reading the *parashiyot* that precede and follow it. Look for poetic passages, parallelism, literary motifs, etc.

2. The *parashah* usually contains passages that beg further study (an odd word, a repetition of some text, the obvious omission of a person, strange behavior by the characters, the narrator's comment, a cryptic commandment, etc.). In addition, each *parashah* is crammed with themes and subjects for discussion.

3. You may want to read from a *Chumash*, which presents commentary that might lead you to interesting passages for further study.

The Books of the Torah

The Torah, also called the Pentateuch and the Five Books of Moses, is the scroll we read in the synagogue. The five books tell the history of the Jewish people, from creation to the death of Moses. They depict the Jewish people's experience of God both as individuals and as a nation. The Torah also sets forth the legal code that Jews continue to live by today.

Genesis (*Bereshit*) begins with the stories of creation and Adam and Eve. It describes the early history of the Hebrews in the time of the patriarchs (Abraham, Isaac, and Jacob) and matriarchs (Sarah, Rebecca, Rachel, and Leah). It tells of Jacob's sons and concludes with Joseph's life and death in Egypt.

Exodus (*Shemot*) describes the slavery of the Jews in Egypt and their redemption under Moses. It tells of the revelation at Mount Sinai, presents the Ten Commandments and other laws, and gives instructions for the building of the Sanctuary in the wilderness.

Leviticus (*Vayikra*) enumerates the priestly laws, as well as laws concerning sacrifices and purity and some civil and criminal laws.

Numbers (*Bemidbar*) continues to describe the Israelites' journey in the wilderness. It tells about the twelve spies who surveyed the land of Canaan and concludes with the Children of Israel poised on the border of the Promised Land.

Deuteronomy (*Devarim*) contains the instructions, laws, warnings, blessings, and curses that Moses delivered to the Israelites immediately preceding his death. It concludes with the death of Moses.

The Parashiyot

Every year we read the Torah from beginning to end, "turning it and turning it again," because each time we read it we learn or understand more than before. In order to make this reading and rereading manageable, the Torah has traditionally been divided into fifty-four individually named *parashiyot*, which are publicly read during synagogue services. Each *parashah* is traditionally accompanied by an additional selection, called a *haftarah*, which is taken from writings by the prophets and which complements the weekly reading from the Torah. Here is a list of the weekly *parashiyot* and their accompanying *haftarot* in the order in which they are read.

Torah Portion	Verses	Haftarah Portion
Genesis		
Bereshit	Genesis 1:1 – 6:8	Isaiah 42:5 – 43:11
Noach	Genesis 6:9 –1:32	Isaiah 54:1 – 55:5
Lech–Lecha	Genesis 12:1–17:27	Isaiah 40:27– 41:16
Vayera	Genesis 18:1–22:24	II Kings 4:1–37
Chaye Sarah	Genesis 23:1–25:18	I Kings 1:1–31
Toledot	Genesis 25:19–28:9	Malachi 1:1–2:7
Vayetze	Genesis 28:10–32:3	Hosea 12:13–14:10
Vayishlach	Genesis 32:4–36:43	Hosea 11:7–12:12
Vayeshev	Genesis 37:1– 40:23	Amos 2:6–3:8
Miketz	Genesis 41:1– 44:17	I Kings 3:15– 4:1
Vayigash	Genesis 44:18– 47:27	Ezekiel 37:15 –28
Vayechi	Genesis 47:28–50:26	I Kings 2:1–12
Exodus		
Shemot	Exodus 1:1–6:1	Isaiah 27:6–28:13; 29:22–23
Va'era	Exodus 6:2–9:35	Ezekiel 28:25–29:21
Bo	Exodus 10:1–13:16	Jeremiah 46:13–28
Beshalach	Exodus 13:17–17:16	Judges 4:4–5:31
Yitro	Exodus 18:1–20:23	Isaiah 6:1–7:6; 9:5–6
Mishpatim	Exodus 21:1–24:18	Jeremiah 34:8–22; 33:25–26
Terumah	Exodus 25:1–27:19	I Kings 5:26–6:13
Tetzaveh	Exodus 27:20–30:10	Ezekiel 43:10 –27
Ki Tisa	Exodus 30:11–34:35	I Kings 18:1–39
Vayakhel	Exodus 35:1–38:20	I Kings 7:40 –50
Pekude	Exodus 38:21– 40:38	I Kings 7:51–8:21

Leviticus

Vayikra	Leviticus 1:1–5:26	Isaiah 43:21– 44:23
Tzav	Leviticus 6:1–8:36	Jeremiah 7:21–8:3; 9:22–23
Shemini	Leviticus 9:1–11:47	II Samuel 6:1–7:17
Tazria	Leviticus 12:1–13:59	II Kings 4:42–5:19
Metzora	Leviticus14:1–15:33	II Kings 7:3–20
Achare Mot	Leviticus 16:1–18:30	Ezekiel 22:1–19
Kedoshim	Leviticus 19:1–20:27	Amos 9:7–15
Emor	Leviticus 21:1–24:23	Ezekiel 44:15–31
Behar	Leviticus 25:1–26:2	Jeremiah 32:6–27
Bechukotai	Leviticus 26:3–27:34	Jeremiah 16:19–17:14

Numbers

Bemidbar	Numbers 1:1– 4:20	Hosea 2:1–22
Naso	Numbers 4:21–7:89	Judges 13:2–25
Beha'alotecha	Numbers 8:1–12:16	Zechariah 2:14– 4:7
Shelach-Lecha	Numbers 13:1–15:41	Joshua 2:1–24
Korah	Numbers 16:1–18:32	I Samuel 11:14–12:22
Chukat	Numbers 19:1–22:1	Judges 11:1–33
Balak	Numbers 22:2–25:9	Micah 5:6–6:8
Pinchas	Numbers 25:10–30:1	I Kings 18:46–19:21
Matot	Numbers 30:2–32:42	Jeremiah 1:1–2:3
Mas'ey	Numbers 33:1–36:13	Jeremiah 2:4–28; 3:4; 4:1–2

Deuteronomy

Devarim	Deut. 1:1–3:22	Isaiah 1:1–27
Va'etchanan	Deut. 3:23–7:11	Isaiah 40:1–26
Ekev	Deut. 7:12–11:25	Isaiah 49:14–51:3
Re'eh	Deut. 11:26–16:17	Isaiah 54:11–55:5
Shofetim	eut. 16:18–21:9	Isaiah 51:12–52:12
Ki Tetze	Deut. 21:10–25:19	Isaiah 54:1–10
Ki Tavo	Deut. 26:1–29:8	Isaiah 60:1–22
Nitzavim	Deut. 29:9–30:20	Isaiah 61:10–63:9
Vayelech	Deut. 31:1–30	Isaiah 55:6–56:8
Ha'azinu	Deut. 32:1–52	II Samuel 22:1–51
Vezot ha-Berachah	Deut. 33:1–34:12	Joshua 1:1–18

Havdalah

It is thought that *Havdalah*, which means "Separation," originated either as a home ceremony at the end of the Saturday afternoon meal or as a synagogue ceremony celebrating God's creation of light on the first day. Midrash tells us that after Adam was created on the sixth day, he spent Shabbat in the sunshine, exploring his new world. At the end of the day, the sun set. Because darkness terrified Adam, God gave him two stones. When Adam struck the stones together, he made sparks of fire. Thus he was comforted and he prayed to the "One who creates the light of fire." These are the very same words we recite after we have lit the *Havdalah* candle.

Although according to tradition we are permitted to work after we have said the *Amidah* prayer of the *Ma'ariv* service on Saturday night, *Havdalah* marks the formal conclusion of Shabbat and our return to the working week. This service consists of four elements: wine, spices, fire, and the acknowledgment of the division between sacred and ordinary time.

The entire *Havdalah* ceremony takes place while we stand. Just as Shabbat is ushered in with *Kiddush*, which begins with a blessing over wine, so it is ushered out with *Havdalah*, which also begins with a blessing over wine. While wine or grape juice is preferable, another beverage may be used as long as it is not water. The leader raises the cup of wine or grape juice and says:

בָּרוּךְ אַתָּה יְיָ אֱלֹהֵינוּ מֶלֶךְ הָעוֹלָם בּוֹרֵא פְּרִי הַגָּפֶן.

Baruch Atah Adonai Eloheinu Melech ha'olam borei peri hagafen.

Blessed are You, *Adonai* our God, Ruler of the universe, Creator of the fruit of the vine.

The blessing over spices is then recited, after which the leader raises and shakes the spice box, inhales the fragrance that the spices emit, and passes the spice box to all who are present. Whether an antique silver spice box or an orange spiked with cloves is used, the pleasure gained from this act is said to be of comfort to all who are present for having to leave the joy of Shabbat behind. The leader lifts the spice box and says:

בָּרוּךְ אַתָּה יְיָ אֱלֹהֵינוּ מֶלֶךְ הָעוֹלָם בּוֹרֵא מִינֵי בְשָׂמִים.

Baruch Atah Adonai Eloheinu Melech ha'olam borei minei vesamim.

Blessed are You, *Adonai* our God, Ruler of the universe, Creator of all spices.

Next, the blessing for fire is recited. It is customary to examine one's hands or fingernails by the light of the candle, using the light so that the blessing is not uttered in vain. Traditionally, a braided candle is used. The candle should have a minimum of two wicks. The leader holds up the candle and says:

בָּרוּךְ אַתָּה יְיָ אֱלֹהֵינוּ מֶלֶךְ הָעוֹלָם בּוֹרֵא מְאוֹרֵי הָאֵשׁ.

Baruch Atah Adonai Eloheinu Melech Ha'olam borei me'orei ha'esh.

Blessed are You, *Adonai* our God, Ruler of the universe, Creator of the light of fire.

Finally, the *Havdalah* blessing itself is recited. The blessing lists a series of distinctions that God has made between the sacred and the ordinary, light and darkness, and the seventh day of rest and the six days of work. The leader lifts the *Kiddush* cup again and says:

בָּרוּךְ אַתָּה יְיָ אֱלֹהֵינוּ מֶלֶךְ הָעוֹלָם הַמַּבְדִּיל בֵּין קֹדֶשׁ לְחוֹל בֵּין אוֹר לְחשֶׁךְ בֵּין יִשְׂרָאֵל לָעַמִּים בֵּין יוֹם הַשְּׁבִיעִי לְשֵׁשֶׁת יְמֵי הַמַּעֲשֶׂה. בָּרוּךְ אַתָּה יְיָ הַמַּבְדִּיל בֵּין קֹדֶשׁ לְחוֹל.

Baruch Atah Adonai·Eloheinu Melech ha'olam hamavdil ben kodesh lechol ben or lechoshech ben yom hashevi'i lesheshet yemei hama'aseh. Baruch Atah Adonai hamavdil ben kodesh lechol.

Blessed are You, *Adonai* our God, Ruler of the universe, who separates the sacred from the commonplace, light from darkness, the seventh day of rest from the six days of labor. Blessed are You, *Adonai*, who separates the sacred from the commonplace.

The leader then extinguishes the candle in the wine or grape juice, and everyone says *Shavua Tov*, "Good Week," to one another.

What Shabbat Means to Me

. . . . ◆ . . . .

Our focus on Shabbat is on persons, not things. The cacophony of the daily struggle should give way to the symphony of life. On Shabbat we acquire an extra soul that enables us to appreciate more fully our families, friends, and ourselves. We experience the pleasure of being a part of the community of Israel reaching toward perfection.

—PETER S. KNOBEL, ED.
GATES OF THE SEASONS
A GUIDE TO THE JEWISH YEAR

Embracing Shabbat As a Newcomer

Antoinette Matlins

Shabbat and all that it embraces is very special to me. And as one who has discovered Judaism only in recent years, I think Shabbat may even be more important to me in some ways than it is to others.

Having not come from a Jewish family or background, I have sometimes felt like a stranger standing on the outside looking in—more like an observer than a participant. In addition, while I could understand a particular occasion or event intellectually, I often felt I wasn't experiencing it on the same emotional level as were those around me.

Perhaps it is because Shabbat provides me with the means to truly *feel* Jewish that I love Shabbat so much. Knowing that Shabbat is at the very core of Judaism, I find that by observing it, I feel connected to Judaism in a way I don't at any other time. Shabbat provides me with the opportunity to create an experience that is personally relevant and meaningful, while it simultaneously connects me to age-old traditions. It makes me feel that I am not only part of an unbreakable chain but an important link within that chain—a link without which the entire chain would be weakened.

I began to observe Shabbat about fifteen years ago, and now it is so much a part of my life that I can't imagine a week without it. Each Friday, I look forward to putting away my normal workweek worries and cares, knowing that however important they may seem, they can wait until after Shabbat. As I prepare to welcome Shabbat, I turn my thoughts to those things about which I really care. And when the children still lived at home, it was wonderful knowing that we were going to have one meal that we enjoyed sharing together as a family in an unhurried manner.

I enjoy all that Shabbat involves—preparing the meal, setting an especially lovely table (during the summer I take pleasure in making a flower arrangement that shares the center of the table with the *Kiddush* cup and candlesticks), and smelling the challah baking in the oven. I love taking a moment to give *tzedakah*. I love the Shabbat blessings and songs and, whenever possible, sharing Shabbat with family, loved ones, and friends.

One Step at a Time

Looking back, however, I remember that it had not always been like this. The way we observe Shabbat in our home today didn't just happen, and it certainly didn't happen all at once. Rather, it evolved over the years, one step at a time. And it involved a process that made me feel I was creating something I could embrace in a way that made it uniquely mine.

I want to stress the word *creating*. I don't believe there is a right or wrong way to observe Shabbat. I think the important thing is to decide you want to begin to separate this time—this day—from the rest of the week; to seek out ways to help you use this time to turn your thoughts and actions to things that really matter; to sanctify this day and make it "holy."

At the same time, however, I think it is important to keep in mind that the observance of Shabbat is at the very core of Judaism, and its observance— perhaps more than any other observance—identifies us as being Jewish and our home as a Jewish home. For this reason, I believe there is a special place for certain traditions in the observance of Shabbat, and I strongly encourage newcomers to keep an open mind to practices that may seem foreign, uncomfortable, or out-of-sync with modern times. Personally, I found it helpful to learn about the rich and varied traditions from our heritage and what they symbolize. Then, as I began to understand them, I discovered that I wanted to make them part of my own observance. There are many beautiful traditions through which we can find inspiration if only we can avoid turning away from them because they are unfamiliar. A friend once reminded me that everything new is, by definition, unfamiliar and, therefore, uncomfortable; it only becomes familiar—and comfortable—through use and/or practice.

I mention this because I remember how uncomfortable I felt when we first began to observe Shabbat in our home. It wasn't my idea to begin "making" Shabbat. It was something my husband wanted to do, and I really didn't know where to begin. I couldn't speak or read Hebrew, the prayers and songs were foreign to me, and I had no idea what to do. I'm sure many others have experienced exactly what I felt.

Attending Services

It all started after my husband, Stuart, began attending Friday evening services—something he hadn't done during the first four years of our marriage. We were living in New York City, caught up in its fast pace. Because of our respective careers, we had so little time together that every minute counted; as a result, I began meeting him at the temple for evening services. This was my first real exposure to Judaism. I still remember watching the ceremonial lighting of the candles, which I always enjoyed, and listening to the magnificent voice of the cantor. I especially enjoyed hearing him sing the blessing over wine—*Kiddush*. And so it went. Each week I met Stuart on Friday evening at the temple. (Gradually I became interested in Judaism and learning more about it, and I discovered that I really was "Jewish"—but that's another story.) At that point, going to Friday evening services and eventually Saturday morning services was as far as my connection to Judaism went.

One evening after about six months of my attending services, Stuart asked me how I would feel about lighting candles at home with the children after services on Friday night. At that point, I was already beginning to embrace Judaism, and I also understood how important to Stuart this small act of making our home feel more "Jewish" would be. So I told Stuart that I thought it would be nice. I really had no idea how to go about it, and I wasn't sure how the children would react. We began simply with my lighting the candles and saying my own personalized thank you to God in my own way. Because I wasn't comfortable with the Hebrew, I read the English translation of the blessing over candles, after which Stuart sang *Kiddush* while I hummed the melody. The children understood that Friday evening was to be family night and that they were expected to be home that evening for dinner, although they could invite friends to join us. We would talk about the week and issues of interest, and we would just be together.

In the beginning, I wasn't the only one who felt a little uncomfortable with the whole thing: The children were even more uncomfortable. They didn't know what to make of it and didn't understand why we were doing it. Yet they sensed that this was something important to us and something we cared about deeply. They never objected and were always very respectful. What we didn't realize until some time later is how much they were absorbing. One Friday evening when we were out of town, our son (a teenager at the time) had a dinner party for some of his friends, at which time he lit the candles and said *Kiddush*. When our housekeeper told us, we were shocked—and delighted. At a time when few things were clear to him, our son knew one thing for sure: He was Jewish and proud of it.

Gradually, as we became comfortable lighting the candles and saying *Kiddush* (which we were soon doing, with a little loving guidance, in Hebrew), we added and created other Shabbat rituals, such as reading Maimonides' eight degrees of *tzedakah* (see page 25) and passing a *tzedakah* box so that each person would remember those less fortunate (we would decide, as a family, how to allocate the money at the end of the year); sharing an inspirational poem or other reading; saying *Hamotzi* and making sure that we had challah on every Shabbat; and so on. We extended our Shabbat experience to include Saturday by making a conscious decision not to work and not to go shopping on that day and by finding ways to make it special and different from the rest of the week. (In summer I love to spend time in my flower garden on Shabbat because I feel that I am closer to God and God's creation there than in any other place.) Today, twelve years later, we can't believe that we were ever without Shabbat.

Stuart and I no longer live in a major metropolitan city, surrounded by Jewish friends and a large Jewish community. We now live in a rural area, on top of a mountain, where we are usually the only two people observing Shabbat. But each Friday evening, as the sun descends, I prepare for Shabbat. And each Friday evening I have no doubt that I am Jewish.

As I light the candles—an act that has, from the very beginning, been for me the most poignant part of Shabbat—I know that I am Jewish. And even on our isolated mountaintop, I know that I am joining Jewish women in every corner of the earth who are also lighting candles. As I light the Shabbat candles, I know that I am part of the continuum of Jewish life and legacy.

And as I watch the flickering flames, I close my eyes and envision the sun setting around the world. As it does, I see pinpoints of light beginning to encircle it until the entire world is embraced in its glow. I am part of that circle of candlelight, part of the glow and warmth that the lit candles have exuded since Jewish time began.

Thank You, God, for Shabbat.

Shabbat As a Setting for Religious Affirmation

Daniel S. Schechter

I want to talk to you in highly personal terms about Shabbat—what it means to me and how I see it as a setting for religious affirmation and growth. But before I do that, I must speak briefly about how I, as a Jew, view Judaism.

I have struggled to define for myself standards for commitment to my faith. This is not an easy task for me or for anyone. We must study the options that tradition gives us, experiment with them, make choices among them, and appropriate for ourselves those that we feel are meaningful.

To me, it is important that Jews live in "sacred time," observing Shabbat— as well as festivals and High Holy Days—celebrating significant moments in our lives in a Jewishly recognizable manner, making Judaism a presence in our homes and families, and pursuing the knowledge of our heritage.

Through our eyes, we perceive religious imperatives differently than did our predecessors. How does one go about being a practicing Jew today without conforming to a traditional set of religious obligations? Contemporary Jews have often been clear about what we don't do. We have not been as clear about what we want to do or should do.

Each week, Shabbat gives me an occasion to reflect on my life: What are its purposes? What is mundane or ordinary, and what is really meaningful or, in fact, sacred? Shabbat gives me an opportunity to reaffirm for myself our people's historic commitment to freedom and justice. It reminds me of God's covenant with Israel and gives me an opportunity to join with other Jews in celebrating this covenant and rededicating ourselves to keeping our part of the compact. As for Jewish study—which we so frequently and glibly state is fundamental to us—what better time than Shabbat for reading about religious or other Jewish themes?

I try to focus my attention on living Jewishly and differently on Shabbat, looking at that day not only as a release from ordinary weekly pressures and as a time for relaxation and family living but also as an opportunity to think about what is truly important to me and how that should influence my activities in the week ahead.

While I frequently do not accomplish all that I would like to in terms of furthering my Shabbat involvement and observance, I do know that my approach makes sense to and works for me. And I have also learned that for Shabbat to be most meaningful to me, I need a taste of it each day, through

53

prayer, reading, or actions—all steps that build my anticipation of the next Shabbat.

Shabbat is a point on which Jews should focus their attention. The observance of Shabbat has been consistently stressed—although in different forms at different times—with a variety of options for observance and celebration. In our freedom to determine what our own Shabbat observance will be, we are not free to ignore Shabbat, for "How can the Sabbath protect us if we don't protect the Sabbath?"

We can begin by learning about Shabbat and raising our consciousness of it. We can next move on to increments of observance, a little at a time, as we become more knowledgeable and comfortable with them. From consciousness-raising, we can move on to such positive acts as lighting candles, having a festive meal, attending synagogue, planning Shabbat events that we feel— as individuals or as families—are in keeping with Shabbat, and making *Havdalah*.

In other words, when I say Shabbat, I refer to its totality as a concept, and I ask you to consider it in that way for yourselves. Some of what we do on Shabbat we do as individuals; some we undertake as part of a family, congregation, or other group. All our Shabbat observances are, of course, highly personal. This is a legitimate and historic Jewish approach, although many Jews do not think about Shabbat in terms of all these dimensions.

If you have come this far with me, let me ask you some questions that I ask myself: Are we prepared to talk about Shabbat making demands on us? Are we as individuals prepared to engage in Shabbat practices that set us apart? Are we prepared to educate ourselves so that we can make informed choices about the observance of Shabbat? Our answers to these questions may lead to changes in the way we live our lives, in the manner in which our synagogues function, and, indeed, in how we define being a Jew.

Finally, let me cite the perceptive words of the late Rabbi Abraham Joshua Heschel. He stated: "Six days we wrestle with the world, wringing profit from the earth; on the Sabbath we especially care for the need of eternity planted in the soul…. Our constant problem is how to live with people and remain free: how to live with things and remain independent…. The Sabbath gives us this inner liberty."

That, to me, is the lesson of Shabbat.

Shabbat in Classic Texts

Esther Saritzky

"*Shabbat Shalom.* May you experience a Sabbath of peace, my friends." Together you and I are reaching out to share in that precious possession of our people, the Sabbath. This endeavor immediately connects us.

I greet you with the words *Shabbat Shalom* because I believe *shalom* is the most wonderful benefit this celebration brings us. It is peace that is at the heart of the observance of Shabbat. The root of the word *shalom* means to be whole, complete, or sound. That is what Shabbat offers us. The home in which it exists takes on that wholeness, that peace, that completion.

When I was a little girl, my father would gather me up in his arms when he returned home from *shul* at dusk on Friday afternoon, and I would ask him for the same brief story, week after week.

"Tell me about the angels, Papa. I want the angels."

And he would tell me about the angels in his simple Yiddish. "On the eve of the Sabbath, a good angel and an evil angel go with each man from his synagogue to his home. If the home is full of discord and is unclean and if the candles are unlit, the evil angel says, 'May the next Sabbath be just the same.' And the good angel is compelled to say Amen. But if, on arriving home, the man finds peace and harmony, the house clean and neat, the table set and the candles lit, the good angel says, 'May the next Sabbath be just like this one.' And the evil angel is forced to say Amen.

"These two angels are over each of us when we celebrate Shabbat. They place their hands on our head and say, 'For this, you are forgiven all your sins and transgressions.'"

Years later, I learned that this story is from the Talmud and that "transgressions" meant those times when we crossed over the boundaries of acceptable behavior as defined in Torah. The story taught my heart a lesson. It taught me that a shining house, a beautifully set table, and, most of all, a home filled with the Sabbath spirit will reproduce itself over and over again. It taught me that the special effort to bring this celebration into my home was worth every ounce of energy it took.

At this moment, I know what you are feeling. Although you might like to experience a Shabbat for yourself, it seems to be a very hard thing to do, perhaps even overwhelming. At this early stage, wholeness, completion, and *shalom* may seem very far off. But they are not. Let's move toward them together!

There is another Jewish legend that tells about a special river, the Sambatyon. That river flows for six days but stops on the seventh. On the other side live the ten lost tribes of Israel. When one crosses that river, time seems to stop and all is peaceful. That river is a symbol of the division between the ordinary days of the week and the Sabbath day. In some ways, the optimum celebration of Shabbat allows time to stop. For a few hours, we leave the ordinary world behind to celebrate our God. Like God, we, too, rest on the seventh day. For a few hours, the sages of Judaism tell us, we are granted a taste of messianic time—the best of the World to Come.

With knowledge, we can invest the ordinary with holiness on Shabbat. For example, we now know that fish helps combat cholesterol levels. But when we serve a fish course on Shabbat, we are also reminded that fish symbolizes our hope for the coming of the leviathan, a mysterious large sea animal that will feed the righteous in times to come. We also put two *challot* on our Shabbat table. They remind us that the Israelites gathered a double portion of manna in the wilderness for Shabbat so that they would not have to work on the day of rest.

Is such knowledge essential for celebrating the Sabbath? Perhaps not. But thinking about our traditions and telling our children about them connects us to the generations that went before and to the Jews around the world who lift their Shabbat *Kiddush* cups the same way that we lift ours.

So how should we proceed? Let us first learn all we can about the celebration of the Sabbath. There are many books and publications that can help us. Your community may offer classes or workshops that can supplement the material provided in this book.

Let us admit that when we first try some Shabbat practices, we may feel ill at ease, perhaps even embarrassed. But let us agree to accept those feelings and go ahead nonetheless. Newness will fade, and we will soon feel comfortable with these customs.

Let us start from where we are. If you can't bake your own challah, try heating the challah that you bought at the bakery. If you can't sing a blessing, recite it. If you don't like chicken and your favorite meal is chili, then make chili *just* for the Sabbath. Most important, let us not say "Because I can't do everything, I will do nothing." Since you can't do everything at once, try at least one new thing each week.

I close with one last tale. Many generations ago, hired missionaries harassed the Ethiopian Jews by demanding that they name the savior of the Jews. The Ethiopian Jews spoke more wisely than they knew when they answered, "The Sabbath is the savior of the Jews." That is a simple and eternal truth, repeated in many ways throughout our history.

So let us celebrate the Sabbath together, and let us begin now.

Observing Shabbat

Harvey Gordon

Where I came from is important. I was raised in a very lapsed Orthodoxy. Shabbat was extremely dreary and joyless. It was an imposition of restrictions, a lot of "thou shalt nots." I really thought that Shabbat was an affliction upon the pious. It was to be avoided or escaped from at any cost. As soon as I was old enough, I did escape. And, not surprisingly, I have spent most of my life without Shabbat. But during the last five or six years, I have come to realize that I do, indeed, have a deep need for a true Shabbat experience. I do have a hunger for the sacred, and I do believe that this need for the sacred requires the nurture that Shabbat can bring to it.

Shabbat is God's gift to me, but it's not an easy gift for me to accept. It can be compared to the following scenario: Your father calls you in and says, "My son, I'm going to give you this rare Stradivarius violin." You look at him and reply, "Thank you, Dad." But what do you do with the violin if you don't know how to play it? In that case, it's hardly a worthwhile gift. And even if you can pick it up and scratch out a tune, it still will not be a source of great joy to you. Only if you work and practice and are ultimately able to make beautiful music on it does it become a very important and worthwhile gift.

So the question about Shabbat for me is, How can I learn to play? And the answer is the same as for the fiddler: I have to practice. In particular, I have to practice total immersion (with apologies to our Baptist friends) and a different form of awareness. To me, total immersion means a blend of postscriptions and affirmations. My experience of Shabbat is hindered by my having to work. If I have to make rounds or if I have to see a sick patient, my experience of Shabbat is hindered. Any technical study hinders it, whether I'm reading about medicine or anything else that will teach me to manipulate rather than just experience my world. Reading a gripping book of fiction is an impediment. Doing anything competitive, like playing a set of tennis, competes with the Shabbat experience. On the other hand, my Shabbat is enhanced when we light the Shabbat candles and when we make *Kiddush* before Shabbat dinner, even if I'm the only one singing at the table. Certainly going to Friday night services, especially when I'm able to pray, enhances Shabbat.

It is also enhanced by any work that illuminates my sense of a place in the cosmos. The authors might be Jewish. They might be philosophers. The work might be an essay by Stephen J. Gould about the nature of evolution or perhaps a book about quantum mechanics, which discusses the new physics and gives me an understanding of the world that I didn't have before.

I could play music; I could listen to music; I could ride a bicycle; I could go to a museum. If the opportunity presents itself, I could hike. Thinking is very, very important to me, particularly thinking about finitude and my mortality. All these activities help me to be more open to the world. They help me to be in harmony, and they help me to be at peace.

My Shabbat is always fragmented. It's fragmented by the necessity of working. It's fragmented by voluntary violations of Shabbat that I impose upon myself. To me, a great enemy of the Shabbat experience is my sense of time. On the other hand, a sense of timelessness, a sense of the eternal, is a great ally. Now I view Shabbat as an eternal sign of creation and as a continuing process. It's not a remembrance of a past event. Because I want to be able to stand at Sinai, I try to achieve a different kind of awareness. I do this by dissolving my self-consciousness and focusing on the moment.

Now it's a struggle to experience Shabbat not as a link between the week that came before and the week that follows but to detach it from its moorings, letting it float like an island in a timeless sea. But because I think I need to do that, I try to experience the world immediately and directly. This is a very different proposition from my daily life, in which everything is part of a chain of contingencies and self-consciousness is an essential element. During the week, I have to be conscious of myself to live and to pursue a career. But on Shabbat, I try to dissolve my self-consciousness. Instead of thinking of myself praying or looking at a tree or menorah, I just pray or look at the tree or the menorah. The latter is a much more intense experience, and I try to focus on the instant. When I stand and look at a menorah with my entire mind, then the bonds of time begin to slip away and I can sense the eternal. This works best for me at services during the period of silent prayer when, instead of using my brain to pray, I just open myself up and try to absorb all the stimuli in the experience.

I'd like to share an experience that was seminal in my learning about Shabbat. It occurred while I was trekking for several weeks in the hills of Nepal. I suppose that it actually began while I was flying to Nepal. If you have flown across the Pacific, you know that the time zones come one after another and the sun never sets. As time goes by, you lose your orientation. You look out the window and see nothing but a sea, and you have no subjective sense of place—there's only the moment. When this happened to me, the bonds of time began to fray.

We arrived in Nepal, which was exotic beyond my imagination. I just sopped up sounds, smells, feelings, and impressions, all of which were foreign to my day-to-day experience. I did not have to associate them with my ordinary responsibilities or my career. There was no need to do anything. I could just be!

In Nepal, people relate to nature in a very intimate way. (This relationship is not buffered, as it is here, with technology.) There is no medicine that we would consider medicine. There are no modern communications. There's no transportation: People carry things on their backs. Heightening the intensity of that relationship are the awesome Himalayas, the plunging gorges. There's no sense of an individual's power there. Rather, one feels a shared fragility with all of creation.

After about ten days of trekking, my self-consciousness finally began to dissolve. I had really begun to enter that society and no longer felt myself to be just an observer.

I want to talk about the twelfth day I was there. It was early January and cool—about 68 degrees probably. The sky was clear, blue, and cloudless. We had trekked only four hours that day before we made camp. I climbed to the top of a hill by myself. It was perfectly silent. Alone, I sat and looked across a valley at the peaks of the Annapurna mountain range. I was sitting about 6,000 feet above sea level; maybe five miles away, snow-covered mountain peaks reached 25,000 feet into the air. They were absolutely awesome. I didn't think about them. I just looked at them. And suddenly, suddenly I was filled—completely filled—with God's presence. I experienced more than just an appreciation of great beauty: I was filled with a sense of awe. After a few minutes, I recited the *Shema* and then the *Shehecheyanu.*

I realize that moments of peak intensity like that one are very brief. But that experience in Nepal taught me a great deal about Shabbat and its rewards. True, I still fall short of my own aspirations and I still choose to do many activities that do not enhance the Shabbat experience. But I have tasted the sweetness of the sacred, and I must tell you that I long for the return of such moments. Little by little, I'm getting better at doing Shabbat. I just need the discipline to continue to grow.

Shabbat En Route

Paul Stone

It's Shabbat at a remote vacation site, a fly-in fishing camp. We are lighting candles in a log cabin in the wilderness.

Light years from my Orthodox childhood and five years since my return to Judaism, here we are, my wife, Phyllis, a recent convert, and I, newlyweds, with a folding traveler's Shabbat candle holder and a slice of bread, because we don't know how to bake a challah in a wood-burning stove.

I needed a spiritual life after forty years away. The New York City congregation welcomed me and offered me friendship, structure, and method. I attended services, Torah classes, and CLUWS workshops, the latter because of some gentle arm-twisting by friends. These friends, the workshop leaders, became an extended family to me, a single man seeking to return to Judaism.

Forty years. And I'm doing what my mother used to do, only she did not look over her shoulder or pray with embarrassment. It took me some time to feel comfortable, even when I was alone lighting Shabbat candles in strange countries and silent hotel rooms.

As one of her wedding gifts to me, Phyllis scoured antique shops and found a pair of brass candelabra that were the last possession of a woman in a nursing home. My brother Max, in amazement over his worldly brother's return to religion, gave me the candlesticks our mother had used for Shabbat. And I have the traveling set, which, last December in New Guinea, stood alongside the yam Phyllis and I used for a *chanukiah*, into which we bored a new hole each evening of Chanukah for the additional candle.

Yes, I have plenty of equipment, but for me the reality is to recognize my Jewish life on a regular basis. Shabbat makes it clearer for me.

The Silvermans' of Bukovina Philosophy of Shabbes

Naomi Gale and Bernie Silverman

Friday night dinner signals the end of the workweek. It also marks an orderly transition from the hectic bustle, tensions, and problems of the past week.

It is a time of an ingathering of family and friends, new and old, as well as strangers, to come together and break bread. It is a time for all to share thoughts, philosophies, humor, achievements, and ideologies.

It is a time when we honor a special occasion—a birthday, a graduation, a particular achievement. The honoree is allowed to choose his or her favorite menu. This is the only time we deviate from the inevitable chicken.

It is a time when our family and friends know exactly where we are. It has been the strength of our family unity and a central factor in our marriage.

In past years, we gathered together at the elder Silvermans. When this became difficult geographically, we carried on the tradition at our home. We are fortunate that our eldest son, his wife, and our grandchildren are nearby and are almost always with us on Friday. On the rare occasions when we are away, our eldest makes Shabbes, making sure to invite whichever family members are around so that the tradition continues.

After everyone is seated, Naomi remains standing. Bernie gives a Sha with a bang of his hand on the table for quiet. Naomi lights the candles and says the blessing aloud in Hebrew. Then she kisses Bernie and tells him to pass the kiss around the table with a Good Shabbes.

Bernie reads the Sabbath Eve prayers from *Gates of the House: The New Union Home Prayerbook* (which we received from the rabbi when we married). He then invites everyone to join him in saying *Kiddush* over wine. The wine cup is passed around the table and each person drinks from it.

After this, Bernie designates a family member or an honored guest to make the blessing over bread and tells this person to place a hand over the cover on the challah and recite the blessing. The cover is removed and the bread is first passed to Bernie and then to the others. An unmarried person is cautioned not to take the heel, as this may impair his or her chances of getting married.

Slow Rise: Braiding a Tradition

Andee Hochman

It took me twenty-eight years to realize that challah will not rise by itself. I was waiting—the way women are taught to wait—for the perfect conditions. I was waiting for a family that fit some recognizable template, for a partner to share my home, for a synagogue to reach out and enfold me in its Friday night Shabbes ritual, for someone to assign me the task, for challah to spring spontaneously from the rightness of things.

I was behaving the way women are taught to behave, waiting patiently and passively, hoping for someone to endorse my idea, invite me inside, solicit my help, say she was hungry and only challah would do.

But this year I took the ritual into my own hands. I followed my partner's great-grandmother's recipe: six cups of flour, a toss of salt, a well in the center, three eggs, half a cup of oil. When I was finished, there were two braided loaves, brushed with eggs and freckled with poppy seeds, steaming when I broke off the first piece.

Until then, I thought that making challah from scratch was a cultural mystery owned by another generation and that I was not quite deserving of induction into its secrets. After all, my cousins and I grew up in typically assimilated late twentieth-century Jewish homes. I didn't go to Hebrew school. I did not have a bat mitzvah. I know more French and Spanish than Yiddish. Was I Jewish enough to make challah?

The first time I made a challah by myself, the process was pure magic: The yeast burped alive in a bowl of warm water, the eggs and oil and flour suddenly blended smoothly together in a pale yellow mass, and the dough rose slowly under a dish towel. And the shreds of wonder did not disappear the second time or even the twelfth. I push and prod the dough and think of my great-grandfather Samuel in his Philadelphia bakery, tossing a few extra loaves into customers' bags.

But I have to confess that sometimes it's a chore like any other. I mix the dough fast with my left hand, thinking about the deadline for my next article. I tear the dough roughly and wind it into quick, tight braids. I do it anyway, because I am interested in the big picture, in the persistence of a private ritual I've begun. I want that even more than I want to indulge my desire, on any particular afternoon, to make phone calls or take a walk and buy challah at the bakery. Sometime in the course of measuring flour and pinching three strands of dough together, I feel my unruly thoughts slow down and my body settle into the routine, like a carrying tide.

I look forward to interrupting my work on Friday afternoons, making the day different. I like Shabbes and observing the spasms of activity and quiet that make the world. The challah reminds me that while I am a writer, I am also a Jew, the great-granddaughter of a baker, and a human being who needs to rest once in a while.

I wish I could say I am making challah as my mother did before me, as my grandmother did before her. But it wouldn't be true. My mother's one botched attempt at making challah is the stuff of family legend (she and her cousin kept adding powdered sugar instead of white flour). I'm not so much continuing a tradition as searching the cultural tapestry for a bright textured thread and tugging it into my own life.

In that life, I sometimes eat challah alone. Sometimes I share it with my partner, housemates, or friends. I give one loaf to the neighbors across the street; I bring one to a dinner party. Sometimes we're busy and grab hunks of hot bread on our way out the door.

The challah is different each week, depending on the season in which the eggs were laid, the coarseness of the flour, the temperature of the house, the heat in my hands, the tightness of the braid, and what I am thinking as I shape it. Each Friday night is different from the last, no matter how much I try to make it familiar. Continuity does not mean sameness.

When it is time to tear the bread and recite a blessing, I hesitate: *Baruch Atah Adonai Eloheinu Melech ha'olam*…. The Hebrew words comfort me; their sounds are ancient lullabies. But they clash with my sense of the universe, where power and reverence are diffused, a bit to each of us, a bit to the flounder and the Japanese maples, too. There is no king—nor queen, for that matter—in my prayers.

What I'd like to offer, whether anyone hears it or not, is a blessing of my own invention. I'd like to acknowledge the alchemy of tradition and imagination that it takes for me to serve challah to my lover and friends 3,000 miles from the site of Samuel's bakery. I'd like to feel glad for a moment that there are still places on this earth where wheat can grow and farmers can tend it.

The flour sits in the canister. The oven is warm enough for the dough to rise. The sun is three hours away from setting, There is no reason to wait.

A Rhythm in Ritual

Tracy Nathan

When I begin the day on Friday morning, I suddenly become aware that I am anticipating the nearness of Shabbat by the fact that I am humming Jewish songs. Although I continue the frenetic pace of my life, I have already begun to think about slowing down, preparing to pause from the rush of the endless work, manipulations, and creation of the week. If I am feeling overwhelmed by all that I must do, I am tempted to "skip" Shabbat that week. After all, there will always be the next week. But then I think about the second half of *Kiddush*, which recalls the Exodus from Egypt. For me, the greatest freedom is to be able to choose not to participate in the grinding daily commerce of life. For this reason, I have found the observance of Shabbat truly liberating. To have a day when I do not have to take part in the constant struggle for achievement or run endless errands provides me with the time and space to enjoy the company of friends or the chance for quiet reading and thinking, removing some of the barriers to spiritual depth and wholeness.

I have always been a person who needs and appreciates markers that set off special times and spaces. In martial arts, one bows as one enters and leaves the space designated as a dojo. The formal gesture marks a boundary and symbolizes the process of leaving the mundane behind. In his beautiful and powerful book on the Sabbath, Abraham Joshua Heschel writes, "There is no danger of its becoming a disembodied spirit, for the spirit of the Sabbath must always be in accord with actual deeds, with definite actions and abstentions. The real and the spiritual are one, like body and soul in a living man. It is for the law to clear the path; it is for the soul to sense the spirit." To prepare for the holy day of Shabbat, I do what generations of Jews have done throughout the centuries. I clean my apartment, put fresh linens on my bed, and make sure there are flowers or something beautiful present so that my home reflects the day's worth. Even if no one will be visiting, it is important for me to feel dignified in my surroundings and to honor the approaching day. Clearing away the physical clutter helps me clear a space so that something different can happen—a chance for spiritual renewal. After a hectic Friday, I walk to the synagogue, eager to join my community in welcoming the Sabbath bride. I feel a stirring within me as we begin to sing *Lechah Dodi*, and my thoughts turn to all the Jews around the world and through the centuries who have welcomed Shabbat with this song.

For my soul to experience the sanctity of the Shabbat day and of life, I have found that it is not enough for me to intellectualize the ideals of rest, freedom, and holiness embodied in the observance of Shabbat: I need to experience them through the body, through actions. That is why I have begun to change my lifestyle and make it move more easily within the rhythm of Shabbat. I choose to walk the twenty-five minutes it takes to get to the synagogue because that helps me slow down my normal rapid pace and avoid the dark underground activity of the subway. I no longer feel comfortable spending money on Shabbat because money, for better or for worse, is the essential lubricant of our public and private lives during the week. It is an extraordinary feeling to discover that it is unnecessary to spend money for twenty-four whole hours. Finally, I always allot a little time for reading something that will nourish me and help keep me focused on the day.

Celebrating Shabbat has created a steady rhythm to my weeks and year. I have come to anticipate the punctuation in the week, the separation from the fierce and driving pursuits of life. And I have also begun to appreciate how the meaning of Shabbat ripples outward: The celebration of Shabbat each week makes all the holy days of the year more meaningful. Now, when I observe Shabbat, I cherish the notion that throughout the world, Jews are reading and studying the same Torah portion and singing many of the same psalms. My communal and personal expression connects me in a very real and profound way to Jews throughout the world, those who are living and those who have come before.

GLOSSARY

A

Ashkenazic Pertaining to Jews of Central and Eastern European background.

B

Birkat Hamazon A blessing of thanks recited after meals.

C

Challah A braided bread traditionally eaten on Shabbat by Ashkenazic Jews.

Chumash The Five Books of Moses; the Torah.

H

Hadlakat Nerot Lighting candles.

Halachah Rabbinic law.

Havdalah Separation. This prayer marks the differentiation between Shabbat and the rest of the week.

Hiddur mitzvah Beautifying the commandment.

K

Kabbalat Shabbat Welcoming Shabbat; psalms, readings, and songs that welcome the Sabbath; the introductory portion of the Sabbath Eve service.

Kabbalists The seventeenth-century mystics of Safed, Israel.

Kiddush The blessings recited or chanted over wine on Shabbat and festivals, emphasizing their holiness.

Kippah A head covering; the Yiddish term is *yarmulke*.

M

Ma'ariv The daily evening prayer.

Midrash A story that illustrates or interprets a Jewish text.

Minchah The daily afternoon prayer.

Mitzvah A commandment; a religious precept or obligation.

N

Netilat Yadayim Washing of hands.

O

Oneg Shabbat "Joy of Shabbat"; a reception after Friday night services, which includes refreshments, socializing, and sometimes a discussion.

P

Parashah (Parashiyot) The weekly Torah portion; also known by the Aramaic word *sidrah*.

S

Sephardic Pertaining to Jews from the Eastern Mediterranean, the Middle East, Caucasus and Central Asia, India, North Africa, and the Maghreb.

Se'udah shelishit The third meal within the twenty-five-hour Sabbath cycle, eaten late on Shabbat afternoon.

Shabbat The seventh day of the week, a day of rest; also called Shabbes.

Shacharit The daily morning prayer.

Shalom Peace; hello; good-bye.

Shamor Keep; observe.

Shehecheyanu The blessing for beginnings and other happy occasions.

Sidrah The weekly Torah portion; also called *parashah*.

T

Talmud The collected legal and ethical discussions of the rabbis; also known as the Oral Law, although it has been written down.

Torah The Five Books of Moses; the Law of Moses.

Tzedakah Justice or righteousness; includes the setting aside of money on Shabbat to be used for the benefit of others.

Z

Zachor Remember.

Zemirot Songs; special hymns sung on Shabbat.

BIBLIOGRAPHY

Call your nearest large city's Jewish bookstore or the publishers listed on pp. 72–74. Addresses and phone numbers are included whenever possible.

For Children

Aronin, Ben. *The Secret of the Sabbath Fish*. Philadelphia: The Jewish Publication Society, 1979.

Bogot, Howard I. *Yoni*. New York: UAHC Press, 1982.

Bogot, Howard I. et al. *Gates of Wonder: A Prayerbook for Very Young Children*. New York: CCAR Press, 1989.

Bogot, Howard I., and Syme, Daniel B. *Prayer Is Reaching*. New York: UAHC Press, 1982.

Brinn, Ruth Esrig. *Jewish Holiday Crafts for Little Hands*. Rockville, MD: Kar-Ben Copies, Inc., 1993.

Burstein, Chaya. *The Jewish Kids Catalog*. Philadelphia: The Jewish Publication Society, 1983.

Cedarbaum, Sophia N. A *First Book of Jewish Holidays*. New York: UAHC Press, 1984.

Fischman, Joyce. *Holiday Work and Play*. Rev. ed. New York: UAHC Press, 1986.

_____. *Let's Learn about Jewish Symbols*. New York: UAHC Press, 1969.

Gellman, Ellie. *Shai's Shabbat Walk*. Rockville, MD: Kar-Ben Copies, Inc., 1985.

Greenberg, Melanie Hope. *Blessings: Our Jewish Ceremonies*. Philadelphia: The Jewish Publication Society, 1995.

Jaffe, Nina. *The Uninvited Guest and Other Jewish Holiday Tales*. New York: Scholastic, Inc., 1993.

Kahn, Janus. *Shabbat Fun for Little Hands*. Rockville, MD: Kar-Ben Copies, Inc., 1994.

Lemelman, Martin. *My Jewish Home*. New York: UAHC Press, 1988.

Nathan, Joan. *The Children's Jewish Holiday Kitchen*. New York: Schocken Books, 1987.

Pomerantz, Barbara. *Who Will Lead Kiddush?* New York: UAHC Press, 1985.

Rosenberg, Amye. *Tzedakah*. West Orange, NJ: Behrman House, 1979.

Sasso, Sandy E. *God's Paintbrush*. Woodstock, VT: Jewish Lights Publishing, 1992.

_____. *In God's Name*. Woodstock, VT: Jewish Lights Publishing, 1994.

Schwartz, Amy. *Mrs. Moskowitz & the Sabbath Candlesticks*. Philadelphia: The Jewish Publication Society, 1983.

Silverman, Maida. *My First Book of Jewish Holidays*. New York: Dial Books for Young Readers (A division of Penguin USA), 1994.

Wylen, Stephen M. *The Book of the Jewish Year*. New York: UAHC Press, 1996.

Zwerin, Raymond A., and Marcus, Audrey Friedman. *Shabbat Can Be.* New York: UAHC Press, 1979.

Cookbooks

Angel, Gilda. *Sephardic Holiday Cooking: Recipes and Traditions.* Mount Vernon, NY: Decalogue Books, Inc., 1986.

Avnon, Naf, and Sella, Uri. *So Eat, My Darling: A Guide to the Yiddish Kitchen.* New York: Frederick Fell Publishers, Inc., 1977.

Friedman, Rose. *Jewish Vegetarian Cooking.* San Francisco: Thorsons, SF (A division of Harper San Francisco), 1993.

Ganor, Avi. *A Taste of Israel.* New York: Galahad Books (A division of LDAP, Inc.), 1993.

Greene, Gloria Kaufer. *The Jewish Holiday Cookbook: An International Collection of Recipes and Customs.* New York: Random House, 1985.

Kinderlehrer, Jane. *Cooking Kosher the Natural Way.* Middle Village, NY: Jonathan David Publishers, Inc., 1983.

Nahoum, Aldo. *The Art of Israeli Cooking.* New York: Hippocrene Books, Inc., 1992.

Nash, Helen. *Kosher Cuisine.* Northvale, NJ: Jason Aronson, Inc., 1995.

Nathan, Joan. *Jewish Cooking in America.* New York: Random House, 1997.

_____. *Jewish Holiday Kitchen.* New York: Schocken Books, 1988.

Wasserman, Debra. *The Lowfat Jewish Vegetarian Cookbook.* Baltimore: The Vegetarians Resource Group, 1994.

Zeidler, Judy. *The Gourmet Jewish Cookbook.* New York: William Morrow & Co., Inc., 1988.

Family

Bial, Morrison David. *Your Jewish Child.* New York: UAHC Press, 1978.

Cardozo, Arlene R. *Jewish Family Celebrations.* New York: St. Martin's Press, 1985.

Holidays (Also see Shabbat)

Fox, Karen L., and Miller, Phyllis Zimbler. *Seasons for Celebration.* New York: Berkley Publishing Group, 1992.

Knobel, Peter S., ed. *Gates of the Seasons: A Guide to the Jewish Year.* New York: CCAR Press, 1992.

Renberg, Dalia H. *The Complete Family Guide to Jewish Holidays.* Bellmore, NY: Modan-Adama Books, 1985.

Schauss, Hayyim. *The Jewish Festivals: History & Observance.* New York: UAHC Press, 1987.

Home

Bial, Morrison David. *Liberal Judaism at Home.* New York: UAHC Press, 1971.

Greenberg, Blu. *How to Run a Traditional Jewish Household.* New York: Simon & Schuster, Inc., 1993.

Syme, Daniel B. *The Jewish Home: A Guide for Jewish Living*. New York: UAHC Press, 1988.

Lifestyle and Life Cycles

Adahan, Miriam. *Raising Children to Care: A Jewish Guide to Child Rearing*. New York: Philipp Feldheim, Inc., 1988.

Borowitz, Eugene B. *Liberal Judaism*. New York: UAHC Press, 1984.

Diamant, Anita, and Cooper, Howard. *Living a Jewish Life: A Guide for Starting, Learning, Celebrating, & Parenting*. New York: HarperCollins Publishers, 1991.

Einstein, Stephen J., and Kukoff, Lydia. *Every Person's Guide to Judaism*. New York: UAHC Press, 1989.

Einstein, Stephen J., and Kukoff, Lydia, eds. *Introduction to Judaism*. New York: UAHC Press, 1983.

Greenberg, Blu. *On Women & Judaism: A View from Tradition*. Philadelphia: The Jewish Publication Society, 1983.

Kertzer, Morris N., revised by Lawrence Hoffman. *What Is a Jew?* Old Tappan, NJ: Macmillan Publishing Co., Inc., 1993.

Maslin, Simeon J., ed. *Gates of Mitzvah: A Guide to the Jewish Life Cycle*. New York: CCAR Press, 1979.

Olitzky, Kerry M., and Isaacs, Ronald H. *The How-to Handbook for Jewish Living*. Hoboken, NJ: Ktav Publishing House, Inc., 1993.

Orenstein, Debra, ed. *Lifecycles, vol. 1: Jewish Women on Life Passages &*

Personal Milestones. Woodstock, VT: Jewish Lights Publications, 1994.

_____. *Lifecycles, vol. 2: Jewish Women on Life Themes & Cycles of Meaning*. Woodstock, VT: Jewish Lights Publications, 1996.

Roth, Cecil, and Wigoder, Geoffrey, eds. *Encyclopaedia Judaica*. Philadelphia: Keter Publishing House, 1994.

Shanks, Judy. *A Teacher's Guide to Liberal Judaism*. New York: UAHC Press, 1984.

Strassfeld, Michael and Sharon. *The First Jewish Catalog: A Do-It-Yourself Kit*. Philadelphia: The Jewish Publication Society, 1973.

_____. *The Second Jewish Catalog: Sources and Resources*. Philadelphia: The Jewish Publication Society, 1976.

Waskow, Arthur. *Down to Earth Judaism: Food, Money, Sex & the Rest of Life*. New York: William Morrow & Co., Inc., 1997.

Music

Davidson, C., ed. *Gates of Song: Music of Shabbat Worship*. New York: Transcontinental Music Publications, 1987.

Friedman, Debbie. *Blessings* (songbook and cassette). San Diego: Sounds Write Productions, Inc., 1990.

Jewish Family Productions. *Celebrate With Us: Shabbat* (cassette). San Diego: Sounds Write Productions, Inc., 1989.

Transcontinental Music Publications. *Nashir B'Yachad: We Sing Together* (cassette/compact disc). New York: Transcontinental Music Publications, 1993.

_____. *Shaarei Shabbat* (cassette). New York: Transcontinental Music Publications, 1992.

_____. *Shiron L'Gan* (songbook). New York: Transcontinental Music Publications, 1993.

_____. *Shiron L'Gan* (cassette/compact disc). New York: Transcontinental Music Publications, 1997.

_____. *Shiron L'Noar* (songbook). New York: Transcontinental Music Publications, 1993.

_____. *Shiron L'Noar* (cassette/compact disc). New York: Transcontinental Music Publications, 1995.

_____. *Shiron L'Yeladim* (songbook). New York: Transcontinental Music Publications, 1993.

_____. *Shiron L'Yeladim* (cassette/compact disc). New York: Transcontinental Music Publications, 1995.

Poems and Short Stories

Brin, Ruth F. *Harvest: Collected Poems*. Wyncote, PA: Reconstructionist Press, 1986.

Sadeh, Pinhas. *Jewish Folktales*. New York: Doubleday & Co., Inc. (A division of Bantam Doubleday Dell Publishing Group, Inc.), 1989.

Prayer

Hoffman, Lawrence, ed. *Gates of Understanding, vol.1: Weekdays, Sabbaths and Festivals*. New York: CCAR Press, 1977.

Roseman, Kenneth D. et al. *Gates of Prayer for Young People: Youth and Family Services*. New York: CCAR Press, 1995.

Shapiro, Mark Dov. *Gates of Shabbat: A Guide for Observing Shabbat* (available with cassette). New York: CCAR Press, 1991.

Stern, Chaim, ed. *Gates of the House: The New Union Home Prayerbook*. New York: CCAR Press, 1977.

_____. *Gates of Prayer: The New Union Prayerbook for Weekdays, Sabbaths, and Festivals*. New York: CCAR Press, 1975.

_____. *Gates of Prayer for Shabbat and Weekdays: A Gender Sensitive Prayerbook*. New York: CCAR Press, 1994.

Shabbat

Abrams, Judith Z. *Shabbat: A Family Service*. Rockville, MD: Kar-Ben Copies, Inc., 1992.

Greenberg, Sidney, and Levine, Jonathan D. *Likrat Shabbat*. Bridgeport, CT: Prayer Book Press, Inc., 1997.

Groner, Judye, and Wikler, Madeline. *Shabbat Shalom*. Rockville MD: Kar-Ben Copies, Inc., 1989.

Heschel, A. J. *The Sabbath*. New York: Farrar, Straus & Giroux, 1975.

Palatnik, Lori. *Friday Night and Beyond: The Shabbat Experience Step-by-Step*. Northvale, NJ: Jason Aronson, Inc., 1996.

Peli, Pinchas H. *Shabbat Shalom: A Renewed Encounter with the Sabbath*. New York: Sure Seller, Inc., 1989.

Teutsch, David, ed. *Kol Haneshamah: Shabbat Vehagim*. Wyncote, PA: Reconstructionist Press, 1994.

_____. *Nashir Unevareh: Songs and Grace after Meals*. Wyncote, PA: Reconstructionist Press, 1992.

Tolley, Jackie, ed. *On Our Spiritual Journey: A Creative Shabbat Service*. La Jolla, CA: Women's Institute for Continuing Jewish Education, 1984.

Wolfson, Ron. *The Shabbat Seder (Art of Jewish Living Series)*. New York: Federation of Jewish Mens Clubs, 1985.

Catalogs

California Stitchery
"The Specialty Catalog of Judaic Designs"
6015 Sunnyslope Avenue
Van Nuys, CA 91401-3020
(800) 345-3332
Fax: (818) 781-2120

The Learning Plant
(Books, games, and classroom aids)
P.O. Box 17233
West Palm Beach, FL 33416
(407) 686-9456
Fax: (407) 686-2415

The Source for Everything Jewish
c/o Hamakor Judaica, Inc.
P.O. Box 48836
Niles, IL 60714-0836
Customer Service (708) 966-4040
Fax: (708) 966-4033

Resource Group

The Vegetarians Resource Group
P.O. Box 1463
Baltimore, MD 21203
(410) 366-8343

Publishers/Sources

Behrman House
235 Watchung Avenue
West Orange, NJ 07052
(212) 689-2020
(800) 221-2755

Berkley Publishing Group
200 Madison Avenue
New York, NY 10016
(212) 951-8800

CCAR Press
(Central Conference of American Rabbis)
355 Lexington Avenue
New York, NY 10017
(212) 972-3636

Decalogue Books, Inc.
7 North MacQuesten Parkway
P.O. Box 2212
Mount Vernon, NY 10550
(914) 664-5930

Dial Books for Young Readers
A division of Penguin USA
375 Hudson Street
New York, NY 10014
(212) 366-2000

Doubleday & Co., Inc.
A division of Bantam Doubleday Dell
  Publishing Group, Inc.
1540 Broadway
New York, NY 10036
(212) 354-6500

Farrar, Straus & Giroux
19 Union Square West
New York, NY 10003
(212) 741-6900

Federation of Jewish Mens Clubs
475 Riverside Drive
New York, NY 10115
(212) 749-8100

Frederick Fell Publishers, Inc.
386 Park Avenue South
New York, NY 10016
(212)752-7565

Galahad Books
A division of LDAP, Inc.
386 Park Avenue South, Room 1913
New York, NY 10016
(212) 679-4200

HarperCollins Publishers
10 East 53 Street
New York , NY 10022
(212) 207-7000
(800) 242-7737

Hippocrene Books, Inc.
171 Madison Avenue
New York, NY 10016
(212) 685-4371

Jason Aronson, Inc.
230 Livingston Street
Northvale, NJ 07647
(201) 767-4093
(800) 782-0015

Jewish Lights Publishing
P.O. Box 237
Sunset Farm Offices, Route 4
Woodstock, VT 05091
Credit card orders: (800) 962-4544

The Jewish Publication Society
1930 Chestnut Street
Philadelphia, PA 19103-4599
(215) 564-5925
(800) 234-3151

Jonathan David Publishers, Inc.
68-22 Eliot Avenue
Middle Village, NY 11379
(718) 456-8611

Kar-Ben Copies, Inc.
6800 Tildenwood Lane
Rockville, MD 20852
(301) 984-8733
(800) 4 KARBEN

Keter Publishing House
Distributed by Coronet Books
311 Barnbridge Street
Philadelphia, PA 19147
(215) 925-5083

Ktav Publishing House, Inc.
900 Jefferson Street
Hoboken, NJ 07030
(201) 963-9524

Macmillan Publishing Co., Inc.
Old Tappan Road
Old Tappan, NJ 07675
(800) 223-2336

Modan-Adama Books
P.O. Box 1202
Bellmore, NY 11710-0485
(516) 679-1380

73

Philipp Feldheim, Inc.
96 East Broadway
New York, NY 10022
(212) 925-3180

Prayer Book Press, Inc.
1363 Fairfield Avenue
Bridgeport, CT 06605
(203) 384-2284

Random House
201 East 50 Street
New York, NY 10022
(212) 751-2600
(800) 638-6460
In MD: (800) 492-0782

Reconstructionist Press
Jewish Reconstructionist Federation
1299 Church Road
Wyncote, PA 19095
(215) 887-1988

St. Martin's Press
175 Fifth Avenue
New York, NY 10010
(212) 674-5151
(800) 221-7945

Schocken Books
201 East 50 Street
New York, NY 10022
(212) 751-2600

Scholastic, Inc.
555 Broadway
New York, NY 10003
(212) 343-6100 (call collect)

Simon & Schuster, Inc.
1260 Avenue of the Americas
New York, NY 10020
(212) 698-7000

Sounds Write Productions, Inc.
6685 Norman Lane
San Diego, CA 92120
(619) 697-6120

Sure Seller, Inc.
136 West 22 Street
New York, NY 10011
(212) 633-2022

Thorsons, SF
A division of Harper San Francisco
1160 Battery Street, 3d Floor
San Francisco, CA 94111
(415) 477-4400

Transcontinental Music Publications
633 Third Avenue
New York, NY 10017
(212) 650-4101

UAHC Press
633 Third Avenue
New York, NY 10017
(212) 650-4120
(888) 489 UAHC

William Morrow & Co., Inc.
1350 Avenue of the Americas
New York, NY 10019
(212) 261-6500

Women's Institute for Continuing
    Jewish Education
126 Executive Drive
La Jolla, CA 92037
(619) 442-2666

ADDITIONAL RESOURCES

FOR CHILDREN

Saypol, Judyth Robbins, and Wikler, Madeline. *Come, Let Us Welcome Shabbat.* Rockville, MD: Kar-Ben Copies, Inc., 1978.

PRAYER

Frishman, Elyse D., ed. *Blessings for the Table*. New York: CCAR Press, 1997.

SHALOM ALEICHEM

CANDLE LIGHTING

A.W. Binder

Serenely (♩ = 50)

Ba - ruch a-tah A-do-nai e-lo - hei-nu me-lech ha-o-lam___

___ a - sher ki-d'-sha-nu b'-mitz-vo - tav___ v'-tzi -

va - nu__ l'-had-lik___ neir, l'-had-lik___ neir shel shab - bat.

KIDDUSH

L. Lewandowski

Moderato
mf

Ba - ruch a-tah A-do-nai E-lo - hei-nu me-lech ha-o-

lam bo - rei p'-ri ha-ga - fen. A-mein.

Ba - ruch a-tah A-do-nai E-lo - hei-nu me-lech ha-o-lam a-

sher kid'-sha-nu b'mitz-vo-tav v'-ra-tza va - nu v'-shab-

bat kod-sho b'-a-ha-vah uv'-ra-tzon hin-chi - la-nu zi-ka-

ron l'-ma-a-sei v' - rei sheet; ki hu yom t'-chi-lah l'-

mik-ra-ei ko-desh zei - cher li-tzi - at Mitz - ra -

yim, ki va-nu va-char - ta v'-o-ta-nu ki-dash - ta mi-

kol ha-a - mim, v'-shab-bat kod-she-cha b'-

a-ha-vah uv'-ra - tzon hin-chal-ta - nu. Ba-

ruch a-tah A-do-nai m'-ka - deish ha-shab-bat. A - mein.

SHEHECHEYANU

Traditional

Freely

Ba - ruch a - tah A-do-nai E-lo- hei-nu me-lech ha-o-lam she-

he-che-ya-nu, v'-ki-y'-ma-nu, v'-hi-gi-a-nu laz' - man ha-zeh. A - mein.

SHEHECHEYANU

Tzvika Pik

Easy tempo (♩ = 104)

Ba - ruch a-tah___ A-do-nai E-lo-hei - nu

me-lech ha-o-lam_____ she-he-che - ya-nu, v'-kiy'-ma-nu v'-

hi-gi-a - nu laz'-man ha-zeh.___ Ah___

Ah___ Ah___ A - mein.___

HAMOTZI

S. Adler

Gently moving (♩ = c. 88 -92)

mf

Ha - mo-tzi le-chem min ha-a-retz, We give thanks to
God for bread: Our voi-ces join in song to-geth-er, As our pray'r is
(alt.: joy-ful
hum-bly said: Ba-ruch a-tah A-do-nai e-lo-hei-nu me-lech ha-o-
pray'r is)
lam, ha-mo-tzi le-chem min ha-a-retz. A - mein.

Y'DID NEFESH

E. & S. Zweig

Lyrically (♩ = 112)

p

Y' - did ne - fesh av ha-ra-cha-man,—— y' - did
ne - fesh av ha-ra-cha-man, m' - shoch av - d' -

81

cha_____ el r'-tzo — ne — cha

m'-shoch av — d'-cha la, la, la, la, la, la,

el r'-tzo — ne — cha. Ya — rutz_____

av — d'-cha k' — mo a-yal,_____

yish-ta-cha-veh la, la, la, la, la, la, la, la,

el mul ha-da — re — cha.

MAH YAFEH HAYOM

Simply (♩ = 116)   Issachar Miron

Mah ya-feh ha — yom,   Sha — bat sha — lom.

Mah ya - feh ha - yom,——— Sha - bat sha - lom.

Sha - bat, sha - bat— sha - lom. Sha - bat, sha - bat— sha - lom.

Sha - bat, sha - bat— sha - lom, sha - bat sha - lom.

BIRKAT HAMAZON

Traditional

Solo: *All, then Solo on repeat*

Ra - bo - tai n'- va - reich.   Y' - hi sheim A - do - nai m'- vo - rach mei - a -

Solo:

tah v'- ad o - lam.   Bir' - shut ma - ra - nan v'- ra - ba - nan v'- ra - bo - tai

n'- va - reich e - lo - hei - nu she - a - chal - nu mi - she - lo.

All, then Solo on repeat

Ba - ruch E - lo - hei - nu she - a - chal - nu mi - she - lo———

83

uv'-tu-vo cha-yi - nu. Ba-ruch hu u-va-ruch sh'-

mo. Ba - ruch a - tah,— A - do - nai E - lo -

hei - nu, me-lech ha-o - lam, ha - zan et ha-o - lam ku -

lo v'-tu-vo b' - chein— b'-che-sed uv'-ra-cha-mim

hu no-tein le - chem l'-chol ba-sar, ki l'-o - lam chas -

do. Uv'-tu-vo ha-ga-dol ta - mid lo cha-sar la-nu

v' - al yech-sar la-nu ma - zon l'-o - lam va-ed. Ba-a -

vur sh'-mo ha-ga-dol.— Ki hu eil zan um'-far-neis la -

84

kol u-mei-tiv la-kol u-mei-chin ma-zon l'-
chol b'ri-yo-tav a-sher ba-rah. Ba-ruch a-tah A-do-
nai ha-zan et ha-kol. U-v'-
nei Y'-ru-sha-la-yim ir ha-ko-desh bim'-hei-ra b'-ya-
mei-nu. Ba-ruch a-tah A-do-nai bo-
neh v'-ra-cha-mav Y'-ru-sha-la-yim. A-mein.
O-seh sha-lom bim-ro-mav hu ya-a-seh sha-lom, a-
lei-nu v'-al kol Yis-ra-eil v'-i-m'-ru: A-mein. A-do-

nai oz l'-a-mo yi-tein, A-do-

nai y'-va-reich et a-mo——— va-sha-lom.

HAVDALAH B'RACHOT

Traditional

Ba - ruch a-tah A-do-nai E-lo-hei-nu me-lech ha-o-lam bo-

rei——— p' - ri ha - ga - fen.———
rei——— mi - nei v' - sa - mim.———
rei——— m' - o-rei ha - eish.———

HAVDALAH CONCLUDING B'RACHAH

Traditional

Ba - ruch a - tah A - do - nai E - lo -

hei-nu me-lech ha-o-lam, ha-mav-dil bein ko-desh l'-chol bein or— l'-

cho - shech bein yom hash' - vi - i l' - shei - shet y' - mei ha - ma - a -

sei, Ba - ruch a - tah A - do - nai ha - mav -

dil — bein ko - desh — l' - chol. —

HINNEI MAH TOV

M. Jacobson

Hi - nei mah tov u - mah na - im

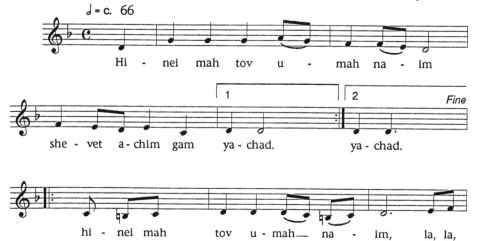

she - vet a - chim gam ya - chad. ya - chad.

hi - nei mah tov u - mah — na - im, la, la,

la, la, la, la, la, la, la, la._____ hi - nei mah tov u-

mah na-im, la, la, la, la, la, la, la, la, la, la, hi - nei mah tov u-

D.C. al Fine

mah na-im_____ she - vet a - chim__ gam__ ya - chad.